OOW

MSE Pocket Book

WITHERBY Seamanship INTERNATIONAL

Witherby Seamanship International
A Division of Witherby Publishing Group Ltd

4 Dunlop Square, Livingston, Edinburgh, EH54 8SB, Scotland, UK

Tel No: +44(0)1506 463 227 - Fax No: +44(0)1506 468 999
Email: info@emailws.com - Web: www.witherbyseamanship.com

First Published 2010
Reprinted 2012
Reprinted 2014

Book ISBN: 978-1-85609-416-0
eBook ISBN: 978-1-85609-417-7

British Library Cataloguing in Publication Data
A catalogue record for this book is available from the British Library.

Printed and bound in Great Britain by Charlesworth Press, Wakefield

Published by
Witherby Publishing Group Ltd
4 Dunlop Square, Livingston,
Edinburgh, EH54 8SB
Scotland, UK

Tel No: +44(0)1506 463 227
Fax No: +44(0)1506 468 999
Email: info@emailws.com
Web: www.witherbys.com

CONTENTS

QUESTIONS

1 Seamanship Class 4 (OOW)

1.1 What types of marine sextant are there?

1.2 What are the three main errors on a sextant?

1.3 When correcting a sextant for errors, is there an order in which they must be corrected?

1.4 What is perpendicularity error?

1.5 What is side error?

1.6 What is index error?

1.7 What fires are foam extinguishers designed for use on, and how?

1.8 How may a fire hose become damaged?

1.9 What are the studs in the anchor cable for?

1.10 How would you secure an anchor for sea?

1.11 What signals may a vessel display to show that it is not safe to fire a rocket?

1.12 When a BA party is entering a space attached to a lifeline, in the absence of voice communication equipment, what signals can they make?

1.13 What pre-donning checks would you make to a positive pressure BA set before wearing?

1.14 Can a lifting plant be used to lift a person?

1.15 When rescuing a casualty from an enclosed space, what are your priorities?

1.16 After a change of more than 25% of the ship's crew, what drills should be held?

1.17 If a substance is described as 'volatile', what does this tell you?

1.18 In the northern hemisphere, if the wind was to veer from South West to West and increase in velocity, together with increasing cloud cover from the west and a falling barometer, what would this indicate?

1.19 What is 'deadweight'?

1.20 What is 'gross tonnage'?

1.21 What is 'net tonnage'?

1.22 How many fire hoses are required to be carried on a vessel?

1.23 How many fire extinguishers are required on a vessel?

1.24 What are the requirements for a deck foam system on an oil tanker?

1.25 What 'bridge' publications are required to be carried onboard UK ships?

1.26 What publications could be referred to for guidance on lashings of cargo?

1.27 When passing information between the bridge and mooring stations, how should verbal instructions be given?

1.28 What information would personnel joining a tanker for the first time receive?

1.29 What mock fire scenarios are to be covered in fire drills?

1.30 What tests can be done to check a hatch cover is watertight?

1.31 Why do we have a 'Permit to Work' system?

1.32 What is a 'Permit to Work System'?

1.33 What sort of work would require a 'Hot Work Permit'?

1.34 What action should you take if, when carrying out work, the fire alarm sounds?

1.35 What is 'Pyrophoric Iron Sulphide'?

1.36 What is the problem with aluminium equipment such as shovels or gangways on tankers?

1.37 How would you secure containers stowed on deck?

1.38 How should pyrotechnics, including line throwing apparatus and distress flares, be disposed of?

1.39 Describe a rescue from an enclosed space.

1.40 What must you be aware of with any 'self-inflating floatation aids' onboard?

1.41 Describe a 'Williamson Turn'.

1.42 A man is seen falling overboard, port side. What actions should you take?

1.43 What precautions would you observe when working a forklift truck in a cargo hold?

1.44 How could you check if you suspect that a vessel is hogged or sagged?

1.45 How would you take a dock-water sample?

1.46 How would you make a slip wire fast to the bitts?

1.47 You are on watch in port where a strong tidal stream is flowing from astern. What mooring would you pay particular attention to?

1.48 Describe how to turn a vessel short round in a river.

1.49 What is a 'fouled anchor'?

1.50 What is a 'fouled hawse'?

1.51 Describe the function of a 'slip wire'?

1.52 What are your immediate actions on boarding a liferaft?

1.53 What type of messages cannot be rejected from a NAVTEX receiver?

1.54 What must you do with an ullage tape before introduction into a tank?

1.55 What are the two key elements of risk used in the context of risk assessment? Where can guidance be found for UK ships?

1.56 You are at anchor in a crowded anchorage and a slick of oil is seen drifting down upon own vessel. What action should you take?

1.57 Name the special areas where the disposal of garbage is prohibited?

1.58 What entries should be made in the 'Garbage Record Book' when garbage is disposed of at sea?

1.59 What are the principles of risk assessment?

1.60 For any given product name, what information would you find about it in the volumes II - IV of the IMDG Code which lists substances Class 1 - 9?

1.61 On a tanker, what options do you have for disposal of retained residues onboard?

1.62 If the ship carries additional safety equipment over and above the statutory required levels, is less maintenance (or reduced maintenance) of that safety equipment required?

1.63 Can the servicing of liferafts exceed 12 months?

1.64 How is the amount a vessel may submerge her load line calculated when loading in a river?

1.65 Explain the transverse thrust effect when an engine with a right-handed propeller is put astern?

1.66 On taking over the watch, what will you be looking for when examining the chart?

1.67 On a tanker with all aft accommodation, what can you expect to happen if the engines are run astern for a period and there is a moderate wind blowing?

1.68 How many extinguisher charge spares are required onboard?

1.69 How many refills are required for foam extinguishers carried onboard?

1.70 What information is on a spare charge for an extinguisher?

1.71 The FFE Regulations state that the number of hydrants shall be such that two jets of water may reach any part of the vessel accessible to passengers or crew. Can this be achieved by the fitting of double hydrants?

1.72 What is the minimum size of a liquid-filled fire extinguisher, foam or water?

1.73 Crew members should participate in one abandon ship drill per month. What should an abandon ship drill consist of?

1.74 Onboard training in the use of LSA should be given to new personnel within two weeks of joining the vessel. What should this involve?

1.75 What information should be contained within a 'Safety Training Log'?

1.76 Can lifeboat falls be replaced before the 5 year requirement?

1.77 Unless liferafts can be 'easily transferred' for launching on either side of the ship, additional rafts should be provided for 150% capacity either side. What does 'easily transferrable' mean?

1.78 A cargo runner has a breaking strain of 3 tonnes. Can it lift a 3 tonne weight?

1.79 When is it not permissible for your vessel to carry dangerous goods?

1.80 During a fire drill, a fire extinguisher does not go off. What action should you take?

1.81 How would you repair a split fire hose?

1.82 How could you forecast fog using the Stevenson Screen?

1.83 How would you differentiate between a Racon and a SART on the Radar?

1.84 Who signs a permit to work before issue?

1.85 You are loading a container and you notice a foul smell coming from it. What action should you take?

1.86 What are the requirements of the hours of work regulation?

1.87 How should the 'hours of rest' periods be allocated?

1.88 Can halon be used as an extinguishing medium onboard?

1.89 What checks would you make when inspecting an inflatable lifejacket?

1.90 Why does the company have a 'Designated Person Ashore'?

1.91 How should the safety induction for new personnel be conducted in port?

1.92 What is a near miss?

1.93 What is a dangerous occurrence?

1.94 You observe a crew member committing what you determine to be an unsafe act. What action should you take?

2 AB and OS Questions

2.1 Can you use a wire rope block with rope?

2.2 Where would you find the correct size of rope to use with a block?

2.3 What marks would you find on a block designed for use with wire rope?

2.4 What maintenance checks would you make on a block?

2.5 How often is lifting machinery to be thoroughly examined?

2.6 How often should a wire rope be inspected?

2.7 When is a wire rope to be condemned?

2.8 How many tucks are required in a wire rope splice?

2.9 You are on a vessel with a derrick. How would you secure a topping lift purchase on bitts or a cleat?

2.10 You are using a synthetic mooring rope, what construction should the stopper be?

2.11 What are the characteristics of 'sisal rope'?

2.12 What are the characteristics of 'hemp'?

2.13 What are the characteristics of 'cotton rope'?

2.14 You are fixing a cotton braided rope to the flag halyards on the christmas tree. Would you use cotton braid on the pull rope for the ship's whistle?

2.15 What are the characteristics of 'polypropylene rope'?

2.16 What are the characteristics of 'polythene rope'?

2.17 What are the characteristics of 'nylon and terylene ropes'?

2.18 What are the characteristics of 'coir rope'?

2.19 If a rope is described as 'hawser laid' what does this denote?

2.20 If a rope is described as 'shroud laid' what does this denote?

2.21 Describe a 'cable laid rope'.

2.22 Describe a 'plaited rope'.

2.23 Describe 'bolt rope'.

2.24 In general, what do synthetic fibre ropes offer good resistance to?

2.25 In general, what do synthetic fibre ropes offer poor protection to?

2.26 What is the general construction of a 'patent logline' (rope)?

2.27 How many tucks would you put in the eye splice of a 'natural fibre rope'?

2.28 How many tucks in an eye splice of a 'polypropylene rope'?

2.29 Describe steel wire rope construction.

2.30 If a wire rope is described as 6 × 7, what does this mean?

2.31 How should you coil down rope?

2.32 How do you open a new coil of rope?

2.33 Where would you stow fibre ropes?

2.34 What would you use a wire of 6 × 12 construction for?

2.35 Where would you use a wire of 6 × 19 or 6 × 24 construction?

2.36 What is wire of 6 × 37 construction used for?

2.37 What construction is siezing wire and where is it used?

2.38 What uses would a bulldog grip have on a wire?

2.39 When making an eye in a wire rope, how do you attach the bulldog grips?

2.40 When would you use a 'flat siezing'?

2.41 When would you use a 'racking siezing'?

2.42 Where would you use a 'figure of eight knot'?

2.43 Where can a 'reef knot' be used?

2.44 Where is a 'double sheet bend' used?

2.45 Where is a 'clove hitch' used?

2.46 Where is a 'cow hitch' used?

2.47 Where would you use a 'round turn' and two 'half hitches'?

2.48 Where is a 'bowline' used?

2.49 When would you use a 'sheepshank knot'?

2.50 Describe a 'hand leadline'?

2.51 On a hand leadline, from where are depths measured?

2.52 What is normally placed in the cavity at the bottom of the lead?

2.53 When is 'Yo-Yo gear' used?

2.54 When working an 'union purchase rig', what is the Safe Working Load (SWL) on the rig and what angle must never be exceeded when lifting?

2.55 In what order do you fit tarpaulins on a hatchcover?

2.56 After the tarpaulins are laid across the hatchboard covers, how are the tarpaulins secured?

2.57 On a vessel with Mcgregor type steel hatchcovers how are they made watertight?

2.58 As a night watchman on a vessel what would your duties include?

2.59 How should a gangway be rigged in port?

2.60 When splicing, what is the difference between a hard eye and a soft eye?

2.61 Name the compass points between North and East.

2.62 Box the compass between West and North.

2.63 Describe a 'Stuelken derrick'.

2.64 How do you stream a patent logline?

2.65 How would you retrieve a log?

2.66 How is an anchor cable marked?

2.67 What preparations are required for anchoring?

2.68 After lowering the anchor clear of the hawsepipe, how would you let it go?

2.69 What is the minimum pressure you would need in a BA set bottle before use?

2.70 When does the warning signal sound on a BA set?

2.71 When can a ship's lifting plant be loaded in excess of its SWL?

2.72 When lifting a load what should you avoid?

2.73 How many turns should be on a drum end when a wire runner is at maximum extension?

2.74 When changing a winch from single to double gear, what should you do?

2.75 What general operating precautions should be observed when working a union purchase rig?

2.76 Do you know of a direct relationship between the angle between the runners to the load on each wire in a union purchase rig?

2.77 In a union purchase rig, what is the name of the guy rigged between the derrick heads?

2.78 What precautions should be taken when painting overside?

2.79 What safety measures would you take when working a stage overside in port?

2.80 When working a bosun's chair, are hooks allowed for securing?

2.81 When a bosun's chair is used for riding a stay, what part of the shackle should come into contact with the wire?

2.82 When the strain on a rope nears breaking point what difference exists between natural and man-made fibre ropes that could be hazardous?

2.83 What measures should be taken when joining a wire to a rope, such as a rope tail on a mooring wire?

2.84 How do you use a chain stopper on a mooring wire?

2.85 When is a pilot ladder required?

2.86 In addition to a pilot ladder, when is a pilot ladder/accommodation ladder combination required?

2.87 When a pilot ladder/accommodation ladder combination is used, how far must the pilot ladder extend above the bottom platform of the accommodation ladder?

2.88 Who can a pilot ladder be used for?

2.89 Where should you position a pilot ladder?

2.90 What should the steps of a pilot ladder be made of?

2.91 What are the dimensions of a step on a pilot ladder?

2.92 How many replacement steps are permitted on a pilot ladder?

2.93 What are the size of the side ropes?

2.94 What size should the spreaders be and how should they be fitted to a pilot ladder?

2.95 What is spontaneous combustion?

2.96 Immediately before letting go the anchor, what checks should you make?

2.97 What sort of a sling would you use to sling 'railway iron' (or similar cargo)?

2.98 On a BA set, what noise does the warning signal make to indicate you have approximately 10 minutes supply left?

2.99 What prevents the lead pellet, which holds the spile pin of a 'Kenter lugless shackle', from falling out?

2.100 When anchoring, what type of ground is good holding ground?

2.101 As a lookout on the bridge, what would you report?

2.102 How should a 'fire wire' be rigged?

2.103 With reference to the fire triangle what are the basics of fighting a fire?

2.104 What is the function of an 'international shore connection'?

2.105 What is the length of a shackle of anchor cable?

2.106 Fire onboard a vessel can be disastrous. Give examples of common causes of fires onboard.

3 Lifeboat and Liferaft Questions

3.1 What are the requirements for a lifejacket?

3.2 What is the maximum number of persons a lifeboat can carry?

3.3 What emergency situations could require the abandonment of vessels?

3.4 What are the requirements for gravity type falls with regards to load and launching of the lifeboat?

3.5 What are the characteristics of a 'rocket parachute flare'?

3.6 What are the characteristics of a 'hand-held distress flare'?

3.7 What information is required on the nameplate on a lifeboat's stem?

3.8 In addition to the markings on a lifeboat's stem, what other markings are there on a boat's hull?

3.9 How many oars are required in a lifeboat?

3.10 How many crutches are required in a lifeboat?

3.11 How many plugs are required in a lifeboat?

3.12 What bailing appliances are available in the lifeboat?

3.13 What type of compass is fitted in the lifeboat and what graduations does it have?

3.14 What is the 'length of line' on a sea anchor?

3.15 When would you 'stream' a sea anchor?

3.16 What pyrotechnics are carried in a lifeboat?

3.17 When would you use a 'rocket parachute flare' in time of distress?

3.18 When would you use a 'hand-held flare' in time of distress?

3.19 When would you use a 'smoke float' in time of distress?

3.20 When would you issue provisions in a lifeboat?

3.21 Where is the 'safety knife' on a liferaft kept?

3.22 What are the contents of the draw string bag in a liferaft?

3.23 How might you obtain water in a liferaft?

3.24 How should occupants sit in a liferaft?

3.25 What is the maximum number of persons for any liferaft Class I or Class VII?

3.26 In cold climates, what protection measures would be necessary in a liferaft?

3.27 What protection requirements for survival are required in hot climates in a liferaft?

3.28 If you are in a liferaft, when would you eat fish?

3.29 How can you conserve body fluids when in a liferaft?

3.30 What are the requirements for a rescue boat?

3.31 What is the additional requirement on vessels where the liferafts are stowed in a position which is 100 metres from stem or stern?

3.32 On a class VII cargo ship, what is the maximum period in which all survival craft required for abandonment must be capable of being launched with a full complement?

3.33 What is the minimum time that a liferaft must remain afloat in all sea conditions?

3.34 From what height can the liferaft sustain repeated jumps on to it?

3.35 What speed is the liferaft able to sustain when being towed?

3.36 Does a liferaft allow sufficient air when its entrances are closed?

3.37 What is the length of painter on a liferaft?

3.38 What are the requirements of a 'hydrostatic release unit'?

3.39 At what speed can a ship proceed and still be able to launch a lifeboat?

3.40 What are the requirements for a 'lifeboat boarding ladder'?

3.41 What are the requirements for running a lifeboat engine out of water?

3.42 What is the maximum required speed of a lifeboat and when towing a liferaft?

3.43 How much fuel is a lifeboat required to carry?

3.44 How many 'painters' are required in a lifeboat?

3.45 What is the required water ration per person in a lifeboat?

3.46 What food rations would you expect to find in a lifeboat?

3.47 What anti-seasickness measures are available in a lifeboat?

3.48 How many thermal protective aids (TPAs) are to be carried in a lifeboat?

3.49 What self-righting properties, if any, is a totally enclosed lifeboat required to have?

3.50 Under what ship conditions can a freefall lifeboat be launched?

3.51 What are the requirements for a self-contained air support system in a lifeboat and how many minutes of air should it provide?

3.52 What are the protection requirements for a lifeboat water spray system?

3.53 How many immersion suits are required in a rescue boat?

3.54 What are the general requirements for immersion suits?

3.55 In terms of thermal insulation, how effective should an immersion suit be?

3.56 What should the minimum luminous range of a lifejacket light be?

3.57 How many additional lifejackets are required to be carried on a vessel?

3.58 How many lifebuoys should be fitted with lights?

3.59 How many lifebuoys are required to be fitted with self-activating smoke signals?

3.60 What markings are there on a lifebuoy?

3.61 How many lifebuoys are required to be carried on a vessel under 100 metres in length?

3.62 How many lifebuoys are required to be carried on a vessel greater than 200 metres in length?

3.63 What size is a lifebuoy?

3.64 Of what material should a lifebuoy be constructed?

3.65 At what height can a lifebuoy be stowed?

3.66 How many line throwing apparatus (LTA) are required on a ship?

3.67 What distance should the LTA be capable of firing the line?

3.68 How would you row a lifeboat against a seaway?

3.69 Where is a 'senhouse slip' commonly used?

3.70 With what frequency are lifeboats to be manoeuvred in the water?

3.71 If a lifeboat can be used as a rescue boat, can a free-fall lifeboat be used for this purpose?

3.72 What weekly checks of LSA equipment would a ships officers normally do?

3.73 What monthly checks of LSA equipment should be made?

3.74 What are the launching requirements for a rescue boat?

3.75 At what range is a lifeboat light to be visible?

3.76 What information is required in the 'SOLAS Training Manual'?

3.77 How often is a liferaft and release sent ashore for servicing?

3.78 What weekly checks of a liferaft would you carry out?

3.79 What actions should an abandon ship drill include?

3.80 On a muster list, what duties are to be specified?

3.81 When is a muster list to be prepared?

3.82 At what period can you end for end a lifeboat fall?

3.83 At what period do you renew a lifeboat fall?

3.84 What frequencies does an EPIRB operate on?

3.85 How can you maximise the efficiency of a SART transponder?

3.86 For how long (minimum) should a lifejacket light remain visible?

3.87 What are the requirements for a water spray system on a lifeboat?

3.88 What are the responsibilities of a lifeboat coxswain?

3.89 On a lifeboat with sails, why would they be 'reefed'?

3.90 What size are the smallest and largest liferafts?

3.91 How many buoyancy chambers should be fitted to a liferaft?

3.92 How many entrances are required on a liferaft?

3.93 What markings are carried on a liferaft?

3.94 What markings are there on the container of a liferaft?

3.95 What are the advantages of a 'davit-launched liferaft system'?

3.96 What are the requirements for inflatable lifejackets?

3.97 For how long should the self-igniting light on a lifebuoy burn?

3.98 What are the requirements for a self-activating smoke float attached to a lifebuoy?

3.99 Where should the muster list be posted throughout the ship?

3.100 How many different types of release mechanism are permitted for the launching of similar lifecraft onboard the vessel?

3.101 How long is the painter of a ship's lifeboat?

3.102 How long is the tripping line of the sea anchor in a ship's lifeboat?

3.103 What is the function of the buoyant lanyard which is sometimes attached to EPIRBs?

3.104 What drills must crew members participate in each month?

3.105 What does the 'General Emergency Signal' consist of?

3.106 When are you required to hold a drill within 24 hours of leaving port?

3.107 What are the monthly requirements for lifeboats and life-saving equipment?

3.108 What are the requirements for testing lifeboats fitted with water spray systems?

3.109 What load can a lifeboat winch hoist?

3.110 What does 'TEMPSC' mean?

3.111 What action should be taken on hearing the emergency signal?

3.112 How many heaving lines are there in a lifeboat?

3.113 What equipment is provided to assist people in boarding a lifeboat from the water?

3.114 Where in survival craft, would you find details of the rescue signals used by coastguards?

3.115 What fire-fighting capability is there in a lifeboat?

3.116 Where are the instructions for pyrotechnics located?

3.117 How is the abandon ship signal given?

3.118 What are 'tricing pennants'?

3.119 What are the list limits for gravity davits?

3.120 What are 'skids'?

3.121 How would you abandon ship using a davit-launched liferaft?

3.122 How would you abandon ship using a boarding ladder and liferaft?

3.123 What length of painter is there on a davit-launched liferaft?

3.124 How many liferafts and what is the total number of persons that can be evacuated by a davit-type liferaft launching arrangement?

3.125 How would you right a liferaft?

3.126 How would you rescue a man in the water from a liferaft?

3.127 How is drift reduced in a liferaft?

3.128 Which lifeboats require an embarkation ladder?

3.129 What means are provided for holding davit-launched liferafts against the ship's side so that persons may be safely embarked?

3.130 What are the markings on a lifejacket?

3.131 How many spare lifejackets must be carried on a passenger ship?

3.132 On an immersion suit, what are the valves on the legs for?

3.133 What is a thermal protective aid (TPA)?

3.134 Will a lifeboat sink if flooded?

3.135 What location aids are there on a lifejacket?

3.136 How many lights are in/on a lifeboat?

3.137 What parts make up the sea anchor on a lifeboat?

3.138 What happens to a liferaft if the ship sinks?

3.139 What are your initial actions after launching the liferaft?

3.140 What is the difference between the pyrotechnics carried in a lifeboat against that of a liferaft?

3.141 What items are provided in a liferaft repair kit?

3.142 How would you get an injured person into the liferaft from the water?

3.143 In tropical regions, how could you keep cool in the liferaft?

3.144 How can you keep warm in the liferaft?

3.145 How many EPIRBs must be carried onboard?

3.146 How would you know if an EPIRB was transmitting?

3.147 How long will an EPIRB continue to transmit for?

3.148 You see an aircraft passing close by and you believe it to have seen you. Would you switch off the EPIRB?

3.149 What is a SART?

3.150 What signal would a SART show on a searching ship's radar?

3.151 How long does a SART transponder last?

3.152 How many SARTs are carried onboard?

3.153 What is the advantage of free-fall lifeboats over conventional lifeboats?

3.154 Where would a rescue helicopter prefer to operate?

4 Checklists

4.1 What checks would you make prior to arrival in port (the 'In-Port Passage Plan' is already complete)?

4.2 What information would you consult when preparing an 'In-Port Passage Plan'?

4.3 When taking over the navigational watch at sea, what information would you give to your relief or expect to be given?

4.4 You are on a vessel about to receive a pilot by helicopter. Which publication would you refer to and what preparation would you make prior to the arrival of a pilot?

4.5 Aside from the testing of bridge equipment, what other checks/preparations are made on a vessel prior to departure?

4.6 What checks on the bridge equipment would you make prior to departure from port?

4.7 As navigating officer, what would you ensure was available/set up on the bridge several hours before departure?

4.8 What checks would you make on the steering gear prior to departure from port?

4.9 In the event of responding to or participating in a 'search and rescue', what actions would you take?

4.10 In the event of a man-overboard, what actions would be carried out?

4.11 In the event of fire, what actions should be carried out?

4.12 In the event of stranding, what actions should be carried out?

4.13 In the event of an imminent collision or in the event of a collision, what actions should be carried out?

4.14 In the event of bridge control or telegraph failure, what actions should be carried out?

4.15 In the event of gyro compass failure, what actions should be taken?

4.16 In the event of steering failure, what actions should be carried out?

4.17 In the event of main engine failure, what actions should be carried out?

4.18 What checks/preparations would be made prior to navigation in areas likely to have ice?

4.19 What preparations are made when navigating in restricted visibility?

4.20 What preparations would you make on the bridge, prior to anchoring?

4.21 What general factors would you take into account when planning a coastal passage or a passage through a TSS?

4.22 When on watch deep-sea, what general considerations should be taken regarding the conduct of your passage

4.23 What checks would be made prior to the embarking or disembarking of a pilot?

4.24 Normally at noon, certain equipment is checked, as part of the daily checks of equipment. What would you, as third officer, test before handing the watch over to the second officer?

4.25 What checks would be made prior to heavy weather or in a tropical storm?

4.26 As officer of the watch in port, what information would you pass to your relief?

4.27 When on cargo watch in port, what duties are expected of the duty officer?

4.28 After taking over the watch in port, what issues should you satisfy yourself with?

4.29 You join your next vessel as OOW. It is a vessel you have not sailed on before and are therefore unfamiliar with the bridge equipment/ layout. What would you check prior to departure in order to familiarise yourself?

5 Bridge Instruments

5.1 What data must be recorded on the VDR (Voyage Data Recorder)?

5.2 Describe the basic functional parts of a VDR.

5.3 Describe the Protective Memory Capsule of a VDR system.

5.4 What is the Automatic Identification System (AIS) coverage?

5.5 What does AIS broadcast?

5.6 What are the advantages of AIS?

5.7 What could be the problems of AIS?

5.8 What is the difference between an ECDIS and an ECS?

5.9 Describe the differences between a vector and a raster chart.

5.10 What are the advantages/disadvantages of raster charts?

5.11 What are the advantages/disadvantages of vector charts?

5.12 What are the risks of over-reliance on an ECDIS system?

5.13 What is an Integrated Bridge System?

5.14 What are the advantages of electronic charts versus paper charts?

6 Security

6.1 What are the objectives of the ISPS Code?

6.2 What is a Ship Security Plan (SSP)?

6.3 What are the various security levels under the ISPS Code?

6.4 To which vessels does the ISPS Code apply?

6.5 To which ports does the ISPS Code apply?

6.6 At security level 1, what activities should be carried out, on all ships, in order to identify and take preventative measures against security incidents?

6.7 At security level 2, what additional protective measures should be carried out, on all ships, in order to identify and take preventative measures against security incidents?

6.8 At security level 3, what additional protective measures should be carried out, on all ships, in order to identify and take preventative measures against security incidents?

6.9 When developing and updating the SSP, an essential part of this is the ship security assessment. What should this assessment consist of?

6.10 When submitting an SSP, or amendments to a previously approved plan, what supporting documents should accompany it?

6.11 What measures should an SSP address?

6.12 Records of what activities regarding security should be recorded onboard?

6.13 What are the duties and responsibilities of the SSO?

6.14 How does a port decide what security level should be set?

6.15 What security measures should a port undertake at security level 1?

6.16 What should the initial survey before the ISPS certificate is issued to the ship consist of?

6.17 How many intermediate ISPS Surveys should take place between the initial issue of an ISPS Certificate and the certificate's renewal?

6.18 What should an intermediate survey consist of?

6.19 What is the period of validity of the ISPS Certificate?

6.20 When a security level is set by a government, to whom does it apply?

6.21 When would a government set security level 3?

6.22 How may the maritime administration of a contracting government notify changes in security levels?

6.23 What information, particularly security related, may be required from a ship as a condition of entry into a port?

6.24 What items should a ship security assessment address?

6.25 When preparing a Ship Security Assessment (SSA), what information will the CSO require?

6.26 Which persons, activities, services and operations would be detailed in the Shipboard Security Assessment (SSA) as important to protect?

6.27 Give examples of possible threats or security incidents that should be considered in the SSA.

6.28 What information should the SSP contain?

6.29 What points of access to the ship should be addressed in the SSP?

6.30 What security measures should be established in the SSP to control access to the ship at security level 1?

6.31 At security level 2, what additional security measures should be applied to protect against a heightened risk of a security incident and to ensure higher vigilance and tighter control?

6.32 At security level 3, what security measures for the ship should be taken including those detailed in the SSP?

6.33 The SSP will detail which areas onboard are restricted and should be clearly marked that unauthorised presence within the area constitutes a breach of security. Give examples of these areas.

6.34 What additional security measures should be taken when taking onboard ship's stores?

6.35 With regard to onboard security, what monitoring capabilities could be utilised?

6.36 What training should the SSO receive?

6.37 What ship specific knowledge or training should the SSO receive?

6.38 What security knowledge should all shipboard personnel be aware of?

6.39 What is the purpose of ship security drills?

6.40 How often should ship security drills be conducted?

6.41 How often should exercises, which may include the participation of CSO, Port Facility Security Officers (PFSOs), relevant authorities of contracting governments as well as the SSOs be held?

6.42 Exercises involving CSOs, PFSOs, relevant authorities of contracting governments as well as SSOs, where possible, should take what format?

6.43 Give examples of areas that would be deemed to be 'restricted' under the Port Facility Security Plan (PFSP).

6.44 What information is required in the form of a Declaration of Security between a ship and a port facility?

6.45 Your vessel is about to enter a port where the security level is higher than that set by the maritime administration for your ship. Which security level would you adhere to?

6.46 All ships were are to be provided with a ship security alert system after July 2004. When activated, what should the alert system initiate?

6.47 From where should the ship security alert system be capable of activation?

6.48 When entering the port of a contracting government to the ISPS Code, what information may be requested by that port prior to entry?

6.49 In terms of the reporting requirements from ship to a port regarding security, for how long or how many previously visited ports should the ship keep records?

7 GMDSS

7.1 An example of the MMSI number for a group of ships is:-
a) 025856223.
b) 002585622.
c) 325698711.
d) 332569871.

7.2 In the event of accidently sending a false distress alert you should:
a) Switch off the equipment, no further action required.
b) Inform the person responsible for your vessel.
c) Do nothing.
d) Cancel the alert by notifying the appropriate MRCC/shore station.

7.3 To avoid the possibility of an INMARSAT-C SES missing routine messages:-
a) Inform the nearest LES with a formal message before switching off.
b) Inform the area NCS with a formal message before switching off.
c) Ensure that the SES has an associated EGC receiver.
d) Perform 'Log-out' before switching off.

7.4 Vessels trading in area A3 fitted with MF/HF DSC must keep continuous watch on:
a) VHF Channel 70, 2187.5 kHz, 8414.5 kHz plus one other HF distress frequency.
b) VHF Channel 70, 2187.5 kHz, 2174.5 kHz plus.
c) VHF Channel 70, 2187.5 kHz.
d) VHF Channel 70, 2174.5 kHz 8414.5 kHz plus one other HF distress frequency.

7.5 A ship station causing interference with communications between another mobile station and a coast radio station shall:
a) Change mode of emission.

b) Request the mobile station to cease transmission.
c) Reduce transmitter power.
d) Cease transmission upon the first request of the coast station.

7.6 The GMDSS radio log book is inspected and signed by the ship's Master at what time interval:
a) Every day.
b) Every month.
c) Only after a distress message had been received.
d) Every week.

7.7 The satellite system which provides marine safety information and has no telephony facility is:
a) INMARSAT-A.
b) INMARSAT-B.
c) INMARSAT-C.
d) INMARSAT-M.

7.8 When a ship is called on 2182 kHz, the ship should reply on:
a) 2182 kHz unless otherwise instructed.
b) The coast station broadcast frequency.
c) 2191 kHz unless otherwise instructed.
d) The coast station paired working frequency.

7.9 Communications on port operations channels may NOT include:
a) Public correspondence.
b) Operational handling of vessels.
c) Movement and safety of vessels.
d) The safety of a person in an emergency.

7.10 VHF Channel 6 may be used for:
a) Onboard communications.
b) Supplementary calling when channel 16 is being used for distress.
c) Ship to shore communications.
d) Ship to aircraft engaged in SAR operations.

7.11 Details of NAVTEX transmissions may be found in:

a) ITU Manual for Maritime Mobile and Maritime Mobile-Satellite Services.
b) ITU List of Coast Stations.
c) ALRS Volume 2.
d) ALRS Volume 5.

7.12 GMDSS area A2 is defined as being:

a) Within range of a shore station having VHF DSC.
b) Approximately 100 to 150 miles from the coast.
c) Within range of a shore station having MF DSC.
d) Within range of NAVTEX.

7.13 In Sea Area A2, ships fitted with MF DSC must keep continuous watch on:

a) 2187.5 kHZ plus 8414.5 kHz.
b) 2177 kHz.
c) 2187.5 kHz plus Channel 70.
d) 2187.5 kHz plus 2177 kHz.

7.14 The transmission of public correspondence telephony traffic is permitted:

a) On Port Operation Channels.
b) Through INMARSAT A.
c) On VHF Channel 70.
d) Through INMARSAT C.

7.15 A Network Co-ordination Station (NCS) of the INMARSAT system:

a) Is located at each Land Earth Station.
b) Allocates a free channel to be used for R/T over INMARSAT.
c) Provides compatibility with other MES terminals.
d) Co-ordinates SAR Operations.

7.16 The person who is responsible for carrying out the mandatory GMDSS tests and checks is:

a) The Officer of the Watch.

b) The person responsible for the maintenance of the electronic equipment.
c) A person nominated in Section B of the GMDSS radio log book.
d) The Radio Surveyor.

7.17 VHF (Channel 70) EPIRBs can be fitted on vessels trading:
a) In Areas A1, A2, A3 and A4.
b) In Area A3 only.
c) In Area A4 only.
d) In Area A1 only.

7.18 Which of the following types of message has the highest 'Order of Priority'?
a) Navigation Warning.
b) Medical Assistance.
c) UN Traffic broadcast.
d) Link call.

7.19 When clearing an auto-telex call to a UK coast station, which abbreviation keeps the radiolink open for a follow-on call:
a) GA+.
b) BRK+.
c) MSG+.
d) KKKK.

7.20 DSC international ship-shore routine calls should be made on:
a) 2191 kHz.
b) 2174.5 kHz.
c) 2187.5 kHz.
d) 2189.5 kHz.

7.21 Details of Port operations stations can be found in:
a) ITU List of Radiodetermination and Special Service Stations.
b) ALRS Volume 8.
c) ALRS Volume 5.
d) ITU List of Coast Stations.

7.22 An INMARSAT M terminal could have the identity number:
a) 312478220.
b) 210210441.
c) 633500150.
d) 019546050.

7.23 Write down the procedure and message transmitted on the 8 MHz. band for the following situation:
- Vessel named 'Louames'.
- C/sign MMYG2.
- M id number 232000123.
- Ship is taking in water and listing dangerously, at position 53° 17'N 17° 43'W, Master requests immediate assistance. Number of persons onboard 23, now abandoning to two lifeboats, SART and EPIRB devices have been activated.

7.24 Outline the broadcast procedure a vessel in a sea area A1 would follow after receiving a VHF DSC distress alert from a vessel in the vicinity.

7.25 Write down the procedure and message transmitted on the VHF band for the following situation:
- Vessel named 'Louames'.
- C/sign MMYG2.
- M id No 232000123.
- Vessel is carrying out surveying work involving a 1000 metre towed line from the hours of 0600UTC and 2000UTC on the 20.06, in Latitudes 50° 05'N to 50° 15'N and Longitudes 002° 00'W to 002° 10'W. All vessels requested to keep well clear.

7.26 Identify the category of GMDSS alerts used for the following situations:
a) Man overboard.
b) Channel 70 EPIRB signal received.
c) Tug assistance required.
d) Shuttle tanker approaching FPSO.

7.27 Identify three methods of distress alerting in the INMARSAT C system.

7.28 A GMDSS vessel is fitted with MF/VHF facilities and sailing in an area A3. List the different methods of distress alerting available to the vessel.

7.29
a) State the specific reasons for transmitting a Distress Relay message.
b) What are the broadcasts a GMDSS vessel would give when relaying a distress in the MF band.
c) State the significant difference between sending a DSC Distress Relay on the MF and VHF bands and that on a HF band.

7.30
a) On a ship's 3 cm (X band, 9 Ghz) radar:
   i. What does the appearance of a SART signal indicate?
   ii. As the vessel approaches, describe the change of signals on the display.
b) i. State the purpose of an EPIRB device.
   ii. List the approved GMDSS type EPIRBs.

7.31 Define the following terms:
a) Seelonce Mayday.
b) Seelonce Feenee.
c) Prudonce.
d) Seelonce Distress.

8 Cargo: General Cargo – OOW Level

8.1 If a cargo is liable to taint, what does this mean?

8.2 Give examples of cargoes liable to taint.

8.3 Give examples of a cargo that is liable to taint others.

8.4 When does ship sweat occur?

8.5 When does cargo sweat occur?

8.6 What publication could be referred to for guidance on lashings of cargo?

8.7 What publications can be referred to for carriage of a timber cargo?

8.8 What tests can be done to a hatch cover to check it is watertight?

8.9 What precautions would you observe when working a forklift truck in a cargo hold?

8.10 Would you lift a full tank container with a normal forklift?

8.11 When carrying motor vehicles on a vessel as cargo, what are the requirements for preparation of the vehicle, aside from the requirement to lash the vehicle?

8.12 If a vessel has tween decks, would they require dunnaging?

8.13 Where would you find information on securing vehicles on a RoRo?

8.14 You are loading a container and you notice a foul smell coming from it. Would you load it?

9 Cargo: Dangerous Goods – OOW Level

9.1 What is a substance's flashpoint?

9.2 Name five types of 'dangerous goods'.

9.3 If a substance is described as 'volatile', what does this tell you?

9.4 What is 'auto-ignition'?

9.5 What is 'spontaneous combustion'?

9.6 How long must a label indicating 'dangerous goods' survive under water?

9.7 What general precautions should you observe when loading dangerous goods?

9.8 What is MFAG?

9.9 In the IMDG Code, for substances it mentions how they should be segregated. Give examples.

9.10 For any given product name, name five things that you can find about it in the IMDG Code that lists substances Class 1 - 9?

9.11 What information does the supplement to the IMDG Code contain?

10 Cargo: Bulk – OOW Level

10.1 Prior to the carriage of a cargo of solid bulk, such as iron ore, what IMO publication could you refer to?

10.2 What publication can be referred to prior to the carriage of a grain cargo?

10.3 What publication could be consulted prior to the carriage of a coal cargo?

10.4 Define 'flow moisture point'.

10.5 Identify items of information that you would be supplied with when loading a solid bulk cargo?

10.6 What tests can be done to a hatch cover to check it is watertight?

10.7 Identify various types of grain produce.

10.8 What preparations are made to a hold for the carriage of grain?

10.9 What methods of securing grain in partly-filled compartments are you aware of?

10.10 What are the main causes of moisture content in bulk cargoes?

10.11 Identify hazards associated with coal cargoes.

10.12 On a bulk carrier, what preparations would you make after a discharge of coal before beginning to load grain?

10.13 What is contained in the IMSBC Code?

10.14 What dangers are associated with iron and iron ore cargoes?

11 Cargo: Oil – OOW Level

11.1 When dipping tanks on a tanker, is it okay to use a dip rod on a polypropylene line?

11.2 What is the advantage of a ringmain pipeline system?

11.3 What are the disadvantages of a ringmain pipeline system?

11.4 What are the advantages of a direct line pipeline system?

11.5 What are the disadvantages of a direct line pipeline system?

11.6 What are the advantages of a free flow system?

11.7 What are the disadvantages of a free flow system?

11.8 What are the advantages of a cruciform pipeline system on a tanker?

11.9 What are the disadvantages of a cruciform pipeline system on a tanker?

11.10 What are the advantages of crude oil washing?

11.11 What are the disadvantages of crude oil washing?

11.12 On a tanker, what options do you have for the disposal of retained residues onboard?

11.13 You are OOW on a tanker when a tank starts to overflow. What action would you take?

11.14 What must you do with an ullage tape before introduction into a tank?

11.15 Below what oxygen level (%) is the required delivery from the inert gas system?

11.16 Below what oxygen level must the atmosphere be maintained in the cargo tanks?

11.17 What is the term for the procedure when inerting, when the incoming inert gas mixes with the original tank atmosphere such that when the process continues the concentration of original gas decreases progressively?

11.18 Before washing a tank in an inert atmosphere, a manual check should be made to ensure that the oxygen level is below what percentage?

11.19 What information would personnel joining a tanker for the first time receive?

11.20 Referring to petroleums, which are volatile?

11.21 Referring to petroleums, which are non-volatile?

11.22 What is the problem with aluminium equipment such as shovels or gangways on tankers?

11.23 What are the properties and problems of H_2S?

11.24 What is the function of a pressure/vacuum relief valve in the inert gas system?

12 Cargo: Chemicals – OOW Level

12.1 What is a P&A manual?

12.2 Which gas is the primary medium used for inerting cargo tanks on chemical tankers?

12.3 Nitrogen represents a particular hazard to those using it because it has no ________?

12.4 What arrangements are available on deck in the event of contamination of personnel?

12.5 Before washing a tank in an inert atmosphere, a manual check should be made to ensure that the Oxygen (O_2) level is below what percentage?

12.6 In which guide would you find first aid information to complement the information on the product data sheet?

12.7 Name three recognised symptoms that indicate poisoning.

12.8 Name a corrosive substance that could be carried on a chemical tanker.

12.9 What are the four main groups of chemical tanker cargoes?

12.10 What is the process called when an animal or vegetable oil goes through a decomposition over a period of time?

12.11 Should a ship use a ship/shore bonding cable, yes or no?

12.12 When a chemical tanker is required to carry oil cargoes, which publications would you find guidelines on the use of inert gas?

12.13 Below what O_2 level is the required delivery from the inert gas system?

12.14 What must the percentage of O_2 content remain below in the cargo tanks?

12.15 What is the term for the procedure when inerting, when the incoming inert gas mixes with the original tank atmosphere such that when the process continues, the concentration of original gas decreases progressively?

12.16 How is TLV expressed?

12.17 What is 'SOPEP'?

13 Cargo: LPG – OOW Level

13.1 What arrangements are available on deck in the event of contamination of personnel?

13.2 In which guide would you find first aid information to complement the information on the product data sheet?

13.3 What is the chemical symbol for ammonia?

13.4 What type of cargo pump is commonly used on LPG carriers?

13.5 Which manufacturer's compressors are commonly used onboard?

13.6 What are the IMO tank volume filling limits for gas carriers?

13.7 What is the name for the amount of cargo that is retained onboard to keep the cargo tanks cool on the ballast voyage?

13.8 Is ammonia vapour lighter or heavier than air?

13.9 Is LPG vapour lighter or heavier than air?

13.10 Can you use a canister or filter type respirator in an enclosed space where the oxygen level is 17%?

14 Cargo: LNG – OOW Level

14.1 The containment systems on LNG ships are mainly of four types, what are they?

14.2 On passage, LNG boil-off is used as fuel. What affects the rate of boil-off?

14.3 Normally, the compressors used on LNG ships have shaft seals pressurised with what?

14.4 LNG is the only liquefied gas product allowed by the Gas Codes to be burnt in the ship's boilers. Why is this?

14.5 Older LNG ships were provided with LNG storage tanks for liquid nitrogen. What has this generally been superseded by?

14.6 LNG vessels commonly have submerged motor pumps installed at the bottom of cargo tanks. Why is this?

14.7 How is the boil-off vapour routed from the ship's cargo tanks to the boilers?

14.8 Moss Rosenberg LNG ships are normally fitted with spray lines in the upper part of each tank. What are these used for?

14.9 What is the LFL and UFL for LNG?

14.10 What is the approximate specific gravity (SG) of LNG Liquid?

14.11 At the change of state from liquid to vapour, what would be a typical volumetric expansion of LNG?

14.12 What is the boiling point of LNG at normal atmospheric pressure?

14.13 What is the relationship between Absolute Pressure and Gauge Pressure?

14.14 What causes the visible white plume when CH_4 vents?

14.15 What is the reason for observing the operating pressure of the cargo tanks at sea above approximately 1083 mbar (Abs) or 70 mbar (Gauge) as an operating allowable minimum cargo tank pressure?

14.16 What is the 'closing' time range for the manifold valves and why is close observance to this important?

14.17 When inerting, what must the hydrocarbon content of the atmosphere be reduced to (maximum allowable limit)?

14.18 Before personnel can be allowed to enter a cargo tank, what other trace gases should be tested for?

14.19 What are the real dangers posed by water ingress into the insulated space?

ANSWERS

1 Seamanship Class 4 (OOW)

1.1 There are two types in common use, micrometer and vernier sextants. The difference between the two mainly lies in the method of graduating and reading the arc.

1.2 The three main correctable errors are:

- Perpendicularity error
- side error
- index error.

1.3 Yes, errors should be corrected in the following order:
1st – Perpendicularity error
2nd – Side error
3rd – Index error.

1.4 Perpendicularity error is present if the index mirror is not perpendicular to the plane of the sextant.

1.5 Side error is present if the horizon mirror is not perpendicular to the plane of the sextant.

1.6 The index arm of the sextant must be parallel to the horizon mirror when the index arm is set at zero. If not, then index error is present.

1.7 Foam extinguishers are primarily designed for use on oil fires. The foam should not be discharged into the burning liquid, but instead directed at a vertical structure to allow it to flow gently over the surface, thus forming a seal which prevents the vapours mixing with the atmosphere. In the case of mechanical foam extinguishers do not point the nozzle directly at the oil before activating as water is discharged initially and will create a 'flash'.

1.8 A fire hose can become damaged by:

- Mildew or by chemicals
- dragging round sharp corners

- being trodden on
- sudden changes in pressure
- shutting off too quickly.

1.9 They studs prevent the individual links deforming (stretching) under stress.

1.10 To secure an anchor for sea:
- Check windlass brakes are screwed up tight, the compressors are on and both cables are out of gear
- attach the devil's claw and hawse pipe covers
- cement spurling pipe covers or attach steel plates with proper canvas covers.

1.11 To show that it is not safe to fire a rocket exhibit:
- By day – code flag 'B'
- by night – red light at the masthead
- in poor visibility – whistle signal 'GU'.

1.12 A system of signals are set up by tugging on the lifeline:
1 pull – we advance
2 pulls – we stop
3 pulls – we return.

1.13 Check the following:
1. Visual inspection of the equipment
2. don the face mask
3. open cylinder fully, check contents (80% or more is required)
4. close cylinder, holding breath, the gauge should not drop more than 10 bars in 10 seconds
5. open cylinder valve, breathing several times to check demand and exhalation valves
6. close cylinder valve and breathe, as air is being consumed whistle must sound between 40-45 bars.

1.14 A lifting plant can be used to lift personnel only if it is designed for this purpose or in an emergency.

1.15 Priorities in rescuing an enclosed space casualty are:

- Restoration of their air supply at the earliest opportunity, and
- unless the casualty is gravely injured, such as a broken back, removal from the space as quickly as possible.

1.16 If more than 25% of the crew have changed and have not participated in a drill in the previous month, then an abandon ship and fire drill must be held within 24 hours of leaving port.

1.17 It has a flashpoint below 60°C.

1.18 These are the signs of an approaching depression (low pressure system).

1.19 It is the weight in tonnes of cargo stores, fuel, passengers, crew and their effects which a vessel is able to carry.

1.20 Gross tonnage is the overall size or capacity of a ship, as per the current tonnage convention, ie the total volumetric capacity in m^3.

1.21 It is derived from gross tonnage by deducting non-earning spaces used for crew, navigation, machinery and fuel.

1.22 At least one fire hose for every 30 metres of ship's length, and a minimum of five. The total length of hoses must be greater than 60% of the ship's length.

Each space available to passengers and crew is to be capable of being reached by two fire hoses.

1.23 Sufficient number of portable extinguishers are required to place at least one in every part of the vessel, with a minimum of five in a vessel of 100 tons and over.

1.24 The deck foam system on a tanker must:

- Be capable of delivering foam to the entire cargo tank area
- have sufficient foam to ensure at least 20 minutes of foam generation (30 minutes if no inert gas system is fitted)

- have a mixture of water to foam that does not exceed 12:1
- not have less than 4 applicators.

1.25 The following bridge publications are required:
- M Notices
- Mariners' Handbook
- Sailing Directions
- Notices to Mariners
- Nautical Almanac
- Navigational Tables
- List of Radio Signals
- List of Lights
- Tide Tables
- Tidal Stream Atlases
- Operating and maintenance instructions for navigational aids carried onboard ship
- International Code of Signals.

1.26 IMO Code of Safe Practice for Cargo Stowage and Securing and your vessel specific Cargo Securing Manual can be referred to.

1.27 Instructions should always be identified with the ship's name in the instruction.

1.28 Personnel joining a tanker or similar vessel for the first time should receive:
- Basic safety induction to the main hazards associated with the vessel (before or on joining the vessel)
- full job description
- information as specified in the Safety Management System.

1.29 Fire drills are expected to cover:
- Holds or other cargo spaces
- oil, gas or chemical fire
- engine/boiler room
- crew/passenger accommodation
- galleys.

1.30 A hatch cover can be tested by:

- A chalk test of the hatch coaming against the rubber
- when hatches are secured a hose test can be performed
- ultrasonic testing.

1.31 A permit to work system:

- Safeguards personnel performing tasks
- safeguards others who may be affected by their actions
- safeguards the vessel
- meets the requirements of company policy and SMS.

1.32 A permit to work system is:

- A written system to assist identification and control of dangerous tasks
- a means of communication between the head of department, supervisor and worker.

1.33 A hot work permit can be required for:

- Welding, flame cutting and grinding
- use of electrical equipment in an atmosphere it's not certified for use in
- use of powered steel brushes/needle guns
- shot blasting.

1.34 If a fire alarm sounds:

- Cease all work
- make worksite safe
- proceed to muster station.

1.35 In an oxygen-free atmosphere, ie an inerted cargo tank, where the volume of Hydrogen Sulphide (H_2S) gas exceeds that of oxygen, iron oxide (rust) is converted to iron sulphide. If a tank containing this atmosphere mix was opened, the iron sulphide would oxidise back to iron oxide and would be accompanied by the generation of considerable heat, such that individual particles may become incandescent.

1.36 If rubbed across steel they can leave an aluminium smear and this, if is subsequently struck, can cause an incendive spark.

1.37 Containers can be secured on deck by:

- Plate lashing terminals on deck
- secure bottle screws to lashing terminals
- penguin hooks fitted in far diagonal of container
- diagonal rod fitted between penguin hook and turnbuckle and container lashed diagonally
- consult the vessel specific information in the 'Cargo Securing Manual'.

1.38 Pyrotechnics should be disposed of by:

- Returning to supplier via local representative
- returning to a liferaft service station who already have procedures in hand for disposal
- contact coastguard or police who will arrange disposal through a military establishment.

1.39 An enclosed space entry rescue would involve:

- Raise the alarm
- rescue team assembled and the rescue plan implemented. No rescue should be attempted without taking the proper precautions
- rescuers to wear SCBA, protective clothing and a lifeline if necessary. Lifting equipment and medical or first aid equipment should be made ready
- the rescue party should never remove their own masks in an attempt to resucitate a victim while in a space. If necessary, breathing equipment should be brought into the space for the casualty
- speed is essential. Yet, it is vital that precautions are observed or the rescuers themselves may become victims. The rescue team should be trained and organised with a rescue plan to meet all emergencies.

1.40 All self inflating floatation devices must be SOLAS complaint, ie stamped and certified.

1.41 A Williamson Turn is executed by:

- Placing the rudder hard over
- after a deviation from the original course of 60 degrees, put the rudder hard over in the opposite direction.
- when on a heading roughly 20 degrees short of reciprocal course, rudder to midship and steady the vessel on a reciprocal course.

1.42 If a man overboard is sighted on the port side:

- Release lifebuoy with light flare or smoke float
- wheel hard over to port (start 2nd motor)
- MOB marker on EPS, ECDIS, etc
- PA announcement, eg man overboard port side, lookouts, man for wheel, Captain to bridge
- signal 'O' can be made on whistle and flag signal to warn shipping
- by continuing a round turn to bring vessel back to a reciprocal course, this will keep the man on the port side throughout and will bring down the vessel's speed rapidly
- reduce speed on engines
- rescue boat to be made ready.

1.43 In a cargo hold:

- The truck should only be used by a competent person
- the truck should only be used when the ship is in still water and never used when the vessel is in a seaway
- vehicles powered by an internal combustion engine should not be used in an enclosed space unless there is adequate ventilation. The engine should not be left running when vehicle is idle.

1.44 Hagging or sagging can be checked by:

- Non-conformities with the fore and aft draught, when compared with mean draught at midships (check vessel is upright)
- hatch covers not closing properly due to possible strain on coamings
- ballast distributed incorrectly
- check permissible sheer forces between bulkheads
- curves of shear forces/bending moments in stability book/ loading computer, and on HSMS (sensors) in bulk carriers.

1.45 Take samples of water around the ship, keeping well clear of any discharges. An average value of the relative density can be obtained by placing the hydrometer in the sample and spinning it round slightly to break down the surface tension about the stem.

Corrections for water temperature may be applied, but these are usually ignored in practice.

1.46 The wire is passed round the bitts in a figure of '8' rotation. On no account must the eye be passed over the bitt. To prevent the wire springing off the bitts, a lashing is placed holding half of the wires, that have been made fast, together.

1.47 Particular attention should be given to the sternlines and forward springs.

1.48 Initially manoeuvre the vessel to the port side of the channel by:

1) Slow ahead wheel to port
2) Slow ahead wheel amidships
3) Begin the turn
4) Half ahead wheel to starboard
5) Stop, wheel midships, half astern
6) Stop, wheel to starboard, half ahead
7) Full ahead, rudder midships.

1.49 It is when the anchor becomes snagged, caught on submarine cable for example.

1.50 This is caused when anchored using two anchors and the vessel has swung and cables have become crossed.

1.51 A slip wire is a wire passed through the eye on a buoy or quay. Both ends of the wire are made fast onboard the ship enabling it to be released easily, referred to as 'slipping a wire'. It can therefore be retrieved without shore intervention.

1.52 On boarding a liferaft:

- Cut the painter and get clear of ship
- look for and pick up other survivors
- stream the sea anchor (drogue) when clear of ship
- close entrances
- bail out raft and inflate floor as required
- distribute sea-sickness tablets
- read survival instructions.

1.53 The following Navtex messages cannot be rejected:

- Nav warnings
- gale warnings
- initial distress information.

1.54 Ensure that the tape is effectively bonded.

1.55 The likelihood that a hazard may occur and the consequences of that hazard. In UK ships, guidance can be found in the Code of Safe Working Practices for Merchant Seamen.

1.56 If oil is sighted on the water surface:

- Advise the Master
- advise port control - ships have been prosecuted for not reporting an adjacent oil sheen/slick as if they had committed the act themselves
- record it in the Deck Log.

1.57 Annex V (Garbage) Special Areas are:
- Mediterranean Sea
- Baltic Sea
- Black Sea
- Red Sea
- Gulfs area
- North Sea
- Antarctic Ocean
- Wider Caribbean region.

1.58 The following entries are required:
- Date and time
- position of ship (latitude/longitude)
- category of garbage discharged
- estimated amount in m^3
- signature of officer in charge.

1.59 A 'risk assessment' is intended to be a careful examination of what, in the nature of operations, could cause harm, so that decisions can be made as to whether sufficient precautions have been taken or whether further steps should be taken to prevent harm.

The aim is to minimise accidents and ill-health onboard ship.

1.60 IMDG Code information includes:
- Label of Class
- UN number
- explosive limits
- properties
- observations
- packing, stowage and segregation.

1.61 Cargo residues can be disposed of by:
- Pumping residues ashore at the loading terminal
- retaining the residues onboard and loading the next cargo on top of them
- pumping the residues to a slop barge

- retaining the residues onboard, but separate from the new cargo.

1.62 No. It should be entered on the safety plan, the planned maintenance schedule and maintained to the same standard as the statutory equipment.

1.63 Yes, where it appears proper and reasonable, the authority may extend the period to 17 months.

1.64 The Dock Water Allowance DWA can be calculated by:

DWA = (1025 – River Density / 25) × FWA.

1.65 The lower blades of the propeller are deeper and thus more effective than the upper blades, which as they are near the surface passing through water which may be constantly broken thus achieving little 'grip'.

The result of this is a pronounced kick to port causing the vessel's head to swing to starboard.

1.66 When taking the watch, assess the chart for:

- Ship's position and methods obtained to determine it
- verify ETAs at alterations of course during the watch and estimated position at the end of the watch
- check the track is laid off correctly on any other charts to be used
- note any conspicuous navigational marks expected
- expected tidal stream
- read the Master's night orders and mark on the chart where he expects a call.

1.67 The stern will tend to seek the wind like a weather vane.

1.68 One for each extinguisher carried.

1.69 One for each extinguisher carried.

1.70 The spare charge has the following markings:

- Full weight
- empty weight
- content weight
- test date
- safety standard ID.

1.71 No, this is not permitted.

1.72 A minimum of 9 litres.

1.73 The abandon ship drill should consist of:

- Summoning of passengers and crew to muster station by the alarm signal
- on reporting to the station, prepare for duties as described in the Muster List
- check passengers and crew are suitably dressed
- check that lifejackets are correctly donned
- lower of at least one lifeboat after any necessary preparation for launching
- start and operate the engine
- operation of davits used for liferafts.

1.74 This training should involve:

- Instruction in the use of LSA and survival at sea
- operation and use of ship's liferafts
- problems of hypothermia, first aid treatment of hypothermia and other first aid procedures
- use of LSA in severe weather and severe sea conditions
- onboard training in the use of davit launched liferafts.

1.75 A safety training log should contain:

- Date when musters are held, details of abandon ship drills
- drills using other LSA
- if a drill is not held at an appointed time, details of same and details of muster/training held in it's place.

1.76 Yes, if due to deterioration of the falls.

1.77 Stowed in a position for easy side-to-side transfer on a single open-deck level, ie not carried through accommodation.

1.78 No, the SWL should be observed when working weights.

1.79 DGS cannot be carried:

- If your vessel does not have a document of compliance
- if the shipper does not present you with a dangerous goods declaration.

1.80 The fire extinguisher is still pressurised, so when re-charging, pressure to be released through holes in screw thread, prior to opening. A risk assessment must be completed first.

1.81 A split fire hose can be temporarily repaired by:

- Cropping the end so as not to infringe the minimum length requirement
- re-bind the hose
- pressure test the hose.

1.82 Plot sea surface temperature against dew point temperature. Where they meet, fog will occur.

1.83 The Racon is a "morse code" letter, where as the SART gives a continous line.

1.84 The authorising officer and competent/authorised person sign the permit.

1.85 Reject the container and inform the Chief Officer.

1.86 The hours of work regulations apply to all seafarers, including Masters, employed or engaged in any capacity onboard a seagoing ship.

They provide for a minimum of 10 hours rest in any 24 hour period and 77 hours in any 7-day period and 4 weeks annual paid leave.

Records of hours of rest are to be maintained and produced for inspection and enforcement by a marine administration.

1.87 Hours of rest may be divided into no more than 2 periods, one of which should be at least 6 hours long, and the interval in between should not exceed 14 hours.

1.88 No, halon systems were required to be decommissioned by 31/12/2003.

1.89 Items identified as being particularly important with inflatable lifejackets include, but are not limited to:

- Inspection of straps, buckles and outer cover
- safety harnesses, its stitching and buckles
- abrasion damage to the inflatable lung
- gas inflation cylinder for signs of corrosion
- gas inflation cylinder for tightness of connection to inflation mechanism.

1.90 The 'Designated Person Ashore', as required by the ISM Code, provides a link between the shore-based organisation of the company and the shipboard safety organisation, having access to the highest levels of management.

1.91 This shall include a 'Safety Welcome Note' given to all personnel immediately on joining. As a minimum, this note must contain Name, Lifeboat Station, Fire Station, any vessel specific safety information and a copy of the Company Safety Policy.

1.92 A near miss is an incident not resulting in injury, material damage, environmental damage, or third party damage, but which conceivably could have done, had the circumstances been slightly different.

1.93 A dangerous occurrence is an incident not resulting in injury, but which has caused material, environmental or third party damage.

1.94 If any staff or crew member sees another committing an unsafe act, they should initially attempt to bring it to the attention of the person involved.

The observation should be followed up by informing the ship's Safety Officer of the incident without necessarily naming the individual concerned, dependent on circumstances.

2 AB and OS Answers

2.1 No, blocks are designed for use with wire or with rope, but not both.

2.2 The size of rope for which the block is intended will be stamped on its shell.

2.3 Blocks for use with wire rope are stamped with the SWL, and also the manufacturers name or mark and a serial number corresponding to the number of the test certificate.

2.4 Swivel head fittings, check collar is secure and free from visible defects, that shank is not distorted and will turn freely by hand, but without having excessive clearance

- Binding check for fractures and corrosion
- side and partition plates, check for distortion
- sheaves, examine for cracks, wear in the groove and for wear and slackness in the bush
- axle pins, ensure that pins are secure and do not rotate within the sheave. Check for wear
- lubricate all moving parts
- protect by painting, but do not paint parts that interfere with free movement or chokes any grease points. Do not paint over reference marks.

2.5 They must be thoroughly examined every twelve months.

2.6 Wire rope must be inspected once every three months, and every month if any wire in the rope is broken.

2.7 No wire rope is to be used when there are signs of wear or other defects or, when in any length of eight diameters, the number of visible broken wires exceeds 10% of the total wires.

2.8 Three full tucks plus two tucks with strands halved, all against the lay.

2.9 With three complete round turns followed by four crossing turns, then lash the four crossing turns down.

2.10 The stopper should also be synthetic.

2.11 Sisal is made from the agave plant. It is weaker and cheaper than manilla, and it is a brittle rope where fibres break easily. Sisal is very stiff and difficult to work with especially when wet. Consequently it is often mixed with manilla to form a composite line.

2.12 Made from the hemp plant, it is normally tarred and used for small work. Commonly used for marline and ratline. Marline is, two stranded, left lay and tarred, used for siezing, worming and serving ropes. Lower grade hemp is used for the heart of wire rope.

2.13 Made from the fibres of the cotton plant, often of three strand right lay or of a braided construction. It may be used as a signal halyard, but generally found as an ornamental rope on gangways, etc. The rope is very easily soiled.

2.14 No, cotton can expand as well as shrink due to climate changes. In shrinking, it can pull tight and activate the ship's whistle.

2.15 Polypropylene rope is the lightest of the synthetic ropes. It is 60% stronger than manila, stretches approximately 40% in length, absorbs only 0.1% water and has a melting point of 165°C.

2.16 The strength of polythene rope lies between manila and nylon. It absorbs only 0.01% water, will float almost indefinitely and offers good resistance to abrasion and sunlight.

2.17 Nylon and terylene ropes are made of fibres which make the rope very strong, soft and pliable. The ropes are waterproof, flexible when wet or dry, nearly impervious to rotting and mildew at extremes of temperature and have a low fire risk. Nylon is generally more elastic than terylene, but both demonstrate good properties of elasticity.

2.18 Coir rope is made from coconut fibre, rough to touch, and reddish brown in colour. It is very buoyant and resistant to rot and will stretch 40 - 50% in length, up to twice that if cable laid. Coir is often used for towing and harbour spring lines.

2.19 Hawser laid refers to a three strand rope laid right handed.

2.20 Shroud lay refers to a four stranded rope laid up right handed around a central hart. It has a greater bearing surface area than hawser lay, thus spreading the frictional wear when used on a drum end.

2.21 Cable lay comprises three hawser laid ropes laid left handed. It is very flexible and ideal for use as a towing spring.

2.22 Plaited rope consists of eight or more strands, four of left hand and four of right hand twist. Mainly used for mooring ropes, it is very flexible, stretches little, does not kink and grips well on winch drums.

2.23 Bolt rope is good quality 3-strand right hand hemp, soft laid for strengthening the edges of sails.

2.24 Synthetic fibre offer good resistance to alkalis, refined oils, organic solvents and rot.

2.25 Synthetic fibres generally offer poor resistance to acids, crude oil, paint and rust remover.

2.26 Patent loglines are normally constructed of very good quality plaited hemp, 10 mm in diameter, sometimes with a stainless steel or copper wire core.

2.27 A minimum of three full tucks.

2.28 Three full tucks. The tucked strands are to be left with tails at least three diameters long.

2.29 Nearly all wire ropes used at sea comprise strands laid right handed over a hemp heart.

2.30 It means a rope of six strands, each having seven wires.

2.31 Normally, the leadline and logline on a ship are the only left hand laid ropes. All others, being right hand laid, should be coiled down right handed.

2.32 Use a turntable and take the rope from the outside of the coil. In the case of small rope sizes, place the coil so that when the end is taken from inside the coil, it will come away anti-clockwise. It may be necessary to pull the end up through the centre of the coil, in which case cut the lashings of the rope, but leave the outer wrapping in place.

2.33 Stow fibre ropes on gratings, not on bare steel decks or with wire ropes. Stow in a dry, well ventilated space away from heat sources such as steampipes. It should be protected from sunlight, even when stowed on deck between ports, rain and ice.

2.34 General purpose and lashing wire. It is flexible, but not as strong as other constructions.

2.35 Flexible wire for running gear such as cargo runners or topping lifts.

2.36 A 6 × 37 wire is used for lifeboat falls.

2.37 Seizing wire is 6 × 1 construction and is used for siezings on wire rope and mousings on shackles or hooks.

2.38 They can be used for making an eye.

2.39 Always fit the grips with the base plate on the working part of the rope and the 'U' bolt around the dead end, using at least three bulldog grips.

2.40 It is used where the strain on both ropes is in the same direction. About ten turns round both ropes, finished off with two frapping turns. Used 'above steps' of a pilot ladder.

2.41 It is used when the strain or pull on two ropes is in opposite directions. Figure of eight turns are made around the ropes, finished off with a frapping. Used below each step of a pilot ladder.

2.42 A figure of eight knot is used to prevent a rope unreeving through a block. It is not as likely to jam as an overhand knot.

2.43 A reef knot is used to join two ropes of equal size. It is unlikely to slip and is easily released.

2.44 A double sheet bend joins two ropes of unequal size and is used for securing a gantline to the bridle of a Bosun's chair.

2.45 A clove hitch provides a quick method of securing a line to a rail. It is likely to jam or if used on a spar that is free to rotate it may pull out.

2.46 A cow hitch the lowering hitch on a Bosun's chair and also used when putting a chain stopper on a wire.

2.47 A round turn and two half hitches is used to secure the end of a rope, as it will not slip and does not readily jam. Commonly used to secure a line from a small boat to a ring on a pier.

2.48 A bowline is used for making a temporary eye in the end of a rope, as it will not slip or jam.

2.49 A sheepshank is used to temporarily shorten a rope. The two smaller bights protruding from the half hitches should be stopped down to the standing part after some weight has been applied to the rope. Commonly found on keel grablines.

2.50 The hand leadline is used to ascertain the depth of water and type of bottom. It consists of about 25 fathoms of hand laid left handed hemp of 10 mm with a 7lb lead and is divided in to nine marks.

Tallow is inserted into the indentation on the bottom of the lead to identity the sea bottom type.

2.51 Depths are marked from the end of the eye. This means the ship will have the benefit of the lead, which is not included in the depths.

2.52 The cavity at the bottom of the lead can be armed with a mixture of white lead and tallow to give an indication of the type of bottom.

2.53 Yo-Yo gear can be used if the weight to be lifted exceeds the SWL of one derrick. Two derricks are doubled together and then placed so the derrick heads are close together. The floating blocks are shackled to the ends of a wire sling which is led through the travelling block.

2.54 The SWL must not exceed one third of the SWL of the derricks or the lowest rated derrick. An angle of 120 degrees must never be exceeded between the runners because, at that angle, the load on each runner will equal the load being lifted.

2.55 Three tarpaulins are spread in the following order:

1) Oldest
2) Newest
3) Second best.

2.56 Wooden wedges are hammered into cleats along the side coamings from fore to aft and from outboard to inboard. This jams the tarpaulin between the battening iron and the coaming. The long face of the wedge should be against the iron.

2.57 By rubber packing set in a channel on the covers, which seals against the upper edge of the coaming when the hatch is closed. The hatch is then secured by clamps.

2.58 The vessel must be patrolled regularly, paying particular attention to fire prevention and detection. The moorings should be adjusted as required to ensure a safe means of access is maintained between the ship and shore. A note is to be kept of those persons ashore, guard against unauthorised persons and maintain general safety precautions. The ship will have a security (ISPS) plan that you should be aware of and follow.

2.59 The gangway should be:

- Clear of the cargo working area
- well illuminated
- have a lifebuoy and line at the top
- be adjusted for tide trim and freeboard
- manropes to be kept tight
- safety net rigged whenever possible.

2.60 A hard eye has a thimble spliced in the rope but a soft eye and just has the eye of the rope spliced against itself.

2.61 N
N × E
NNE
NE × N
NE
NE × E
ENE
E × N
E

2.62 W
W × N
WNW
NW × W
NW
NW × N
NNW
N × W
N

2.63 The stuelken derrick may have a SWL up to 300 tonnes. The derrick is positioned between two posts and may, on some vessels, serve two hatches by swinging between the posts. Three or four winches may be used, two of which for topping. The derrick is controlled from a single control unit.

2.64 Ship the register, setting pointers to zero, connecting the electric cable.

- Connect the governor to the register with the tail forward
- choose the correct length of logline for the ship's speed
- lead the logline (attach) securing it to the link and rotator
- to stream the log, lower the rotator into the wake and then pay out the logline, placing no undue strain on the register and its mounting.

2.65 To retrieve a log:

- Note the time and readings
- stop the governer and grasp the logline abaft of it, recovering enough line to pass the bight through a fairlead
- disconnect the logline from the governer and the governer from the register
- retrieve the logline
- recover the rotator with care and retrieve the balance of the line
- wash the rotator and smear with light oil. Wash and stow the register and govern
- stow the logline in bights to dry.

2.66 At the end of the first shackle, the first studded link either side of the kenter shackle will have turns of siezing wire wrapped around it. The kenter shackle is painted red and the links either side painted white.

At the second shackle, siezing wire is placed round the second link away from the kenter shackle, the kenter shackle being painted red and the two links either side painted white.

At each subsequent kenter shackle the number of links are marked correspondingly.

2.67 Preparations for anchoring include:
- Power on deck
- take a spike, hammer, crowbar, oil can, goggles and a torch to the focsle
- remove the hawsepipe covers
- with windlass out of gear and brake on, rotate winch slowly oiling moving parts
- put whichever anchor is required in gear
- remove the devils claw and compressor bar
- inform the officer that the anchor is ready for lowering clear of the hawsepipe.

2.68 Once clear of the hawse pipe:
- Walk the anchor to the waterline
- engage brake and disengage gearing
- inform Officer that the anchor is on the brake and ready to let go
- wearing goggles, let the brake go when ordered, braking when required
- when the vessel is 'brought up', put the brake on and, place the compressor bar across the chair
- hoist the anchor ball.

2.69 No less than 80%.

2.70 The warning sounds at 40-45 bar.

2.71 Only for the purpose of carrying out a test.

2.72 It should not be lifted over a person or accessway.

2.73 At least three turns.

2.74 That you land the load before changing gear.

2.75 General operation precautions for a union purchase rig include:

- Angle between the married runners should not exceed 90 degrees, and never 120 degrees
- cargo slings should be kept as short as possible to clear bulwarks and the angle between the runners should be limited
- derricks should be topped as high as possible
- derricks should not be rigged further apart than is absolutely necessary.

2.76 The load is related to the angle between the runners as follows:
At 60 degrees = 1/2 load
at 90 degrees = 3/4 load
at 120 degrees = load
at 175 degrees = 12 × load.

2.77 This is called the schooner guy.

2.78 A lifeline and buoyancy aid should be worn. The operation should be completed under the supervision of a seaman on deck who would have a lifebuoy with a sufficient length of line ready for immediate use.

No work should be undertaken overside while the vessel is underway

2.79 When working a stage overside the following ensure the following:

- Permit to work for overside work
- stage tested and inspected
- the two gantlines used in rigging should be long enough to trail into the water to provide additional lifelines should the operator fall. A lifebuoy and line should be kept ready.

2.80 Yes, but only if they are of a type that cannot be easily dislodged.

2.81 It is essential that the bow of the shackle and not the pin rides on the wire. The pin should also be siezed.

2.82 Natural fibre ropes give no audible warning when approaching breaking point.

2.83 A thimble should be inserted in the eye of the rope and both wire and rope should have the same direction of lay.

2.84 The chain stopper secured by a cow hitch followed by turning up against the lay of the wire to ensure that the chain neither jams nor opens up the lay of the wire.

2.85 A pilot ladder is required when the distance from the water to the point of access on the vessel exceeds 2.5 metres.

2.86 A combination is required when the distance from the water to the point of access exceeds 9 metres.

2.87 The ladder should extend 2 metres above the platform.

2.88 A pilot ladder is only to be used for officials while the ship is arriving at or leaving port or for embarkation/disembarkation of pilots.

2.89 A pilot ladder should be positioned so that it is:

- Clear of discharges from the ship
- clear of fine lines of the hull
- each step rests firmly against the ship's side
- the person using it can gain safe access by climbing not less than 1.5 metres nor more than 9 metres.

2.90 The pilot ladder steps should be made of ash, elm, oak, teak or any other equally strong hardwood or other material of equal strength and durability.

2.91 Steps on a pilot ladder are 48 cms long, 11.5 cms wide and 2.5 cms thick.

2.92 No more than two replacement steps are permitted and these must be replaced as soon as practicable by the original method of securing.

2.93 Side ropes should have a size equal to 18 mm manila.

2.94 Spreaders should be 1.8 to 2.0 metres long, spaced no more than nine steps apart, but the lowest spreader may be fitted on the fifth step from bottom.

2.95 Dirty waste, rags, sawdust and other rubbish, particularly if left contaminated with oil, are dangerous if left lying about. Heat may be generated spontaneously within such rubbish, which may be sufficient to ignite flammable mixtures or become hot enough to set the rubbish itself on fire. Such waste and rubbish should therefore be properly stored until it can safely be disposed of.

2.96 Before letting go the anchor ensure that there are no small craft or obstacles under the bow.

2.97 By use of a chain sling, having a hook at one end and an enlarged link at the other. The chain is passed round the item once or twice and the end hooked round the chain. When lifting, the weight of load tightens the chain round the load.

2.98 The warning is indicated by a whistle noise.

2.99 The lead pellet is inserted into a dovetail recess hole which prevents the pellet from coming adrift.

2.100 Clay, mud or hard sand makes good holding ground.

2.101 A lookout should report the following to the OOW:

- Any lights, vessels or large floating objects seen and, particularly in restricted visibility, any fog signals heard
- although in congested waters every light that is seen could not possibly be reported, report those which are likely to pose a collision risk, especially small craft which may not be observed easily from the bridge.

2.102 On tankers alongside, the fire wires should be hung in positions where the tugs can get to them without difficulty, usually the offshore side. To allow for sufficient wire to be paid out, sufficient slack wire should be retained between the bitts and the fairlead and secured by a rope yarn.

2.103 Fire is extinguished by the removal of heat, fuel or air, each is one side of the fire triangle.

2.104 The international shore connection connects the water supply from the shore to the vessel's firemain. The connection provides a standardised union between the two systems for fighting fires onboard a ship.

2.105 An anchor cable shackle is 15 fathoms (27.5 metres) long.

2.106 Common causes of fire on a ships include:

- Faulty electrical appliances/circuitry
- overloading of electrical circuitry
- careless disposal of cigarette ends
- spontaneous combustion of dirty waste/rags particularly if contaminated with oil
- damp storage of linen/materials
- oil spillage/leakage in machinery spaces
- galley fires due to overheating of cooking oils
- carelessness with hand pressing irons
- incorrect methods of drying laundry.

3 Lifeboat and Liferaft Answers

3.1 A lifejacket should meet the following requirements:

- Constructed to eliminate the possibility of being worn inside out
- capable of turning wearer from any position in still water to the floating position with the wearers body inclined backwards
- mouth of the wearer to be kept 15 cm above the water
- to be made of a highly visible colour
- to be fitted with a whistle and light
- must allow wearer to jump a vertical distance of 6 metres without injury and without dislodgement of jacket.

3.2 A maximum of 150 persons.

3.3 Reasons for abandonment can include explosion, fire, stranding, collision or foundering.

3.4 Capable of launching with a full complement with vessel listed up to 15 degrees either way. The boat falls should be long enough to reach the water with the vessel at her lightest sea-going draught and listed 15 degrees either way.

3.5 Rocket parachute flares should produce a red star of luminosity of 30,000 candela, rise to a minimum height of 300 metres and fall at a minimum rate of 5 metres/second.

3.6 A hand flare should show a red light of minimum intensity of 15,000 candela and remain lit for a minimum of 1 minute.

3.7 Lifeboats are required to have the following information on the stem:

- Number of persons
- dimensions of the boat
- surveyor's initials
- certifying authority's stamp.

3.8 The following are also required:

- Strips of retroreflective tape
- the name and port of registry of the ship to which the lifeboat belongs
- number to show which side of the lifeboat the lifeboat belongs.

3.9 1 full set and 2 spare oars are required.

3.10 One and a half sets of crutches are required.

3.11 Two plugs are required for each hole in the lifeboat.

3.12 Bailing appliances that are required:

- Manual pump
- two 9 litre buckets
- one bailer of at least 8" diameter.

3.13 Liquid compass with half point graduations is required.

3.14 A sea anchor, drogue, should be three times the length of the boat.

3.15 A sea anchor or drogue should be streamend:

- When you want to stay in the same area
- to keep the vessel's head into the wind
- when beaching.

3.16 A lifeboat carries the following pyrotechnics:

- 4 rocket parachute flares
- 6 hand-held flares
- 2 smoke floats.

3.17 At night when land or ships are 15 - 40 miles away.

3.18 By day or night when object is 5 - 10 miles away.

3.19 In visual range by day and for alerting aircraft.

3.20 24 hours after abandoning at regular intervals, such as morning/noon/evening. Water may be issued earlier if any person has sustained injuries or fluid loss.

3.21 In a pouch inside the liferaft access.

3.22 The contents are:
- Topping-up foot pump
- torch
- spare batteries
- bulbs
- leak stoppers 1, 3 + 5
- table of life-saving signals
- spare sea anchor
- repair kit.

3.23 In a liferaft water can be obtained from:
- Tins or sachets of drinking water
- catchment pockets
- solar still/desalination.

3.24 Survivors should sit round the edges with feet in the middle and their arms through the straps.

3.25 A maximum of 25 persons.

3.26 In a liferaft in cold climates:
- Inflate the floor
- keep warm and dry, huddling together if necessary
- ventilation should be adjusted to the minimum required
- basic exercise of limbs such as moving toes and fingers to avoid cold injury.

3.27 In a liferaft in hot climates:
- Proper ventilation, avoiding sunburn
- reduce the need for water by no unnecessary movements including swimming
- maintain a through breeze
- keep the outside of the raft wet.

3.28 Protein type foods such as fish require large quantities of water to enable the digestion process, so do not eat fish unless water is abundant.

3.29 Water can be conserved by:
- Eat the daily food ration provided
- take seasick remedy
- rest and avoid unnecessary exercise
- shelter from the sun in hot climates
- ensure adequate ventilation.

3.30 The requirements for a rescue boat include:
- Able to carry at least 5 persons seated and 1 stretcher
- capable of travelling at 6 knots for 4 hours
- towing arrangement must be fitted
- all equipment secured except boat hooks, which are to be kept free for fending off
- searchlight, radar reflector, TPAs for 10% or a minimum of 2, whichever is the lesser
- if inflatable, to remain inflated
- it should be capable of being recovered at speeds up to 6 knots.

3.31 In addition to the liferafts required, a liferaft carried as far forward or aft as practicable is necessary. It may be securely fastened so to permit manual release and need not be of the type that can be launched from an approved launching device.

3.32 They must be ready for launch in 10 minutes.

3.33 The liferaft must remain afloat for 30 days in all sea conditions.

3.34 Repeated jumps can be sustained from 4.5 metres.

3.35 A liferaft can be towed at 3 knots in calm water when laden with its full complement of persons and equipment and one of its sea anchors streamed.

3.36 Yes, it shall admit sufficient air for the occupants at all times even with the entrances closed.

3.37 A painter must not be less than twice the distance from the stowed position to the waterline in the lightest sea-going condition or 15 metres, whichever is greater.

3.38 A hydrostatic release unit (HRU) should:

- Be constructed of materials to prevent malfunction of the unit
- automatically release the raft at a depth of 4 metres
- have drains to prevent the build up of water in the hydrostatic unit
- be so constructed as to prevent release when seas wash over the unit
- be permanently marked on its exterior with its type and serial number
- be such that each part connected to the painter system has a strength of not less than that required for the painter.

3.39 A lifeboat must be capable of being launched while the ship is making headway at 5 knots.

3.40 Lifeboats shall have a boarding ladder that can be used on either side of the lifeboat to enable persons in the water to board the lifeboat. The lowest step of the ladder shall not be less than 0.4 metres below the lifeboat's lightest waterline.

3.41 The engine shall be capable of running out of water for no less than 5 minutes after starting from cold with the lifeboat out of the water.

3.42 The maximum required speed of a lifeboat is 6 knots in calm water and 2 knots when towing a 25 man liferaft.

3.43 Sufficient fuel is carried to run a fully laden lifeboat at 6 knots for 24 hours.

3.44 Two painters of equal length that are twice the distance from the stowage position of the lifeboat to the waterline.

3.45 The lifeboat is to carry a total of 3 litres per person for each person of which 1 litre per person may be replaced by a de-salting apparatus, capable of producing an equal amount of water in 2 days.

3.46 There is to be a food ration of no less than 10,000 kj for each person. These rations shall be kept in airtight packaging and stowed in a watertight container.

3.47 Six doses of anti-seasickness medicine and one seasickness bag for each person.

3.48 The lifeboat must carry either 2 TPAs or a number that equals 10% of the number of persons the lifeboat is permitted to carry, whichever is greater.

3.49 The stability of the lifeboat shall be such that it is inherently or automatically self-righting when loaded with a full or partial complement of persons and equipment, all entrances and openings are closed watertight, and the persons are secured with safety belts.

3.50 With the ship in its lightest sea-going condition, under unfavourable conditions, trimmed up to 10 degrees and with the ship listed not less than 20 degrees either way.

3.51 The system must operate when proceeding with all entrances and openings closed, the air in the lifeboat to remain safe and breathable and the engine running normally for a period of no less than 10 minutes. During this time the pressure inside the lifeboat shall never fall below that outside, nor shall it exceed it by more than 20 Pa (mb).

3.52 A lifeboat water spray system should be capable of protecting the number of persons the lifeboat is required to carry when subjected to a continuous oil fire enveloping the lifeboat for a minimum period of 8 minutes.

3.53 An immersion suit is required for every person assigned to crew the rescue boat.

3.54 An immersion suit shall be constructed with waterproof materials such that:

- It can be unpacked and donned without assistance within 2 minutes
- it will not sustain burning or continue melting after being totally enveloped in a fire for a period of 2 seconds
- it will cover the whole body with the exception of the face. hands shall be covered unless permanently attached gloves are provided
- it is provided with an arrangement to minimise or reduce the amount of free air in the legs of the suit
- following a jump from 4.5 metres into the water, there is no ingress of water in to the suit.

3.55 An immersion suit with no inherent insulation and is designed to be worn in conjunction with warm clothing, should ensure that the body's core temperature does not drop more than 2°C when immersed for an hour in water at a temperature of 5°C.

An immersion suit with inherent insulation shall ensure that the body's core temperature does not fall more than 2°C after a period of 6 hours immersion at water of a temperature of between 0 and 2°C.

3.56 A lifejacket light should have a luminous range of at least 1 mile.

3.57 On a vessel of more than 16 persons, 25% additional lifejackets are required.

3.58 No less than half the total number onboard.

3.59 Two, which must be capable of quick release from the wheelhouse.

3.60 Each lifebuoy shall be marked in block capitals with the name and port of registry of the ship on which it is carried.

3.61 8 lifebuoys are required.

3.62 14 lifebuoys are required.

3.63 A lifebuoy has an outer diameter of no more than 80 cm and inner diameter of no less than 40 cm.

3.64 It should be constructed of inherently buoyant material; it shall not depend upon rushes, cork shavings or granulated cork, any loose granulated material or any air compartment which depends on inflation for buoyancy.

3.65 A lifebuoy is constructed to withstand a drop of 30 metres, or from the height that it is stowed at above the waterline in the lightest sea-going condition, whichever is the greater distance. The drop must not impair the buoys' operating capability or that of its' attached components.

3.66 A unit with four projectiles or four individual (LTAs) must be carried.

3.67 It should be capable of throwing the line at least 230 metres in calm weather.

3.68 When managing a small boat in heavy breaking seas, speed is an important factor. For instance, an increase in speed will carry a boat through or over a breaking crest, but without forward momentum, there may be the possibility of the boat capsizing. You must take care not to proceed too fast or the boat will fall heavily when the crest has passed. By reducing the speed in ample time, the waves will break ahead of the boat.

3.69 Where quick release is necessary, such as the gripes on a lifeboat or the tricing pennants.

3.70 Each lifeboat to be manoeuvred in the water every 3 months. Free-fall lifeboats are to be free-fall launched every 6 months.

3.71 No, a separate rescue boat is required.

3.72 Weekly LSA checks can include:

- Visual inspection of all survival craft and rescue boat and launching appliances
- run lifeboat and rescue boat engines ahead and astern for no less than 3 minutes
- general alarm to be tested.

3.73 Inspection of all LSA equipment, including the lifeboat and rescue boat contents.

3.74 A rescue boat must be capable of launching within 5 minutes in a headway of up to 5 knots.

If also a lifeboat, it should be launched with full rescue equipment or up to 6 persons, whichever is greater.

3.75 A lifeboat light must be visible at 2 miles.

3.76 The SOLAS training manual should include:

- Donning of lifejackets and immersion suits
- mustering
- boarding, launching and clearing survival craft
- method of launching from within the survival craft
- release from launching appliances
- illumination in launching areas
- use of all survival equipment
- use of all detection equipment
- illustration on the use of radio LSA
- use of sea anchors
- use of engines and accessories
- recovery of survival craft and rescue boat
- hazards of exposure and the need for warm clothing
- best use of survival craft facilities
- methods of retrieval, helicopter rescue gear, shore LSA, ship's line throwing apparatus

- all functions contained in the muster list
- instructions for emergency repair of LSA.

3.77 Intervals not exceeding 12 months.

3.78 Check the following weekly:

- Check integrity of the container and lashings
- ensure the painter is secured and not hanging on deck as it can act like a wick bringing moisture into the raft
- sight hydrostatic release.

3.79 An abandon ship drill should include:

- Summoning to muster by means of general alarm
- ensure all understand abandon ship order
- ensure all carry out alloted duties
- ensure all are suitably dressed with lifejackets donned correctly
- prepare and lower at least one lifeboat
- lifeboat engines run.

3.80 The following duties are to be specified on a muster list:

- Closing of openings
- survival craft: preparation, launching and equipping
- muster of passengers
- communication equipment
- fire team manning
- officers responsible for maintenance of LSA/FFE
- substitutions for key personnel.

3.81 A muster list must be prepared before the ship proceeds to sea.

3.82 Lifeboat falls are normally end for ended every 2½ years.

3.83 The lifeboat fall is renewed every 5 years.

3.84 121.5 MHz and 406 MHz.

3.85 By mounting it as high as possible to increase its radar horizon.

3.86 A lifejacket light should remain illuminated for at least 8 hours.

3.87 The requirements of a water spray system are that:

- Water shall be drawn from the sea by a self-priming pump
- it shall be capable of turning on or off the flow of water over the exterior of the lifeboat
- the seawater intake is so arranged as to prevent the intake of flammable liquids from the sea surface
- the system shall be designed to allow flushing with fresh water and complete drainage.

3.88 The responsibilities of a lifeboat coxswain include:

- To check passengers and crew are wearing their lifejackets correctly and secured in the correct manner
- to ensure crew members/passengers are correctly dressed, ie warm clothing/immersion suits
- to check boat and equipment and ensure that they are in good order
- maintain authority and deliver all orders in a clear manner
- to check the overside is clear before the launching the boat
- to carry out a safe launch and take the boat away from the ship's side
- Responsible for the safety of the crew throughout.

3.89 This procedure reduces the sail area should the wind increase, as making way under full sail in strong winds greatly increased the chances of capsize.

3.90 The smallest liferaft is a 6 man and the largest is a 102 man. The 50 man liferaft is normally used in marine evacuation systems, although 102 man rafts are produced by some manufacturers.

3.91 Two, each fitted with a non-return valve and each capable of supporting the full complement of the raft.

3.92 Every raft for more than 8 persons should have at least two entrances, which are diametrically opposite.

3.93 A liferaft requires the following markings:

- Manufacturer's name or trademark
- serial number
- date of manufacture
- name of approving authority
- name and place of servicing authority
- number of persons permitted to carry.

3.94 A liferaft container should have the following markings:

- Manufacturer's name or trademark
- serial number
- name of approving authority
- number of persons raft permitted to carry
- the word 'SOLAS'
- the type of emergency pack enclosed in the raft
- length of painter
- maximum permitted height of stowage above the waterline
- launching instructions.

3.95 Advantages of a davit launched liferaft system include:

- Quick evacuation of personnel
- persons can enter the raft dry
- the davit can be used for release of more than 1 liferaft.

3.96 Inflatable lifejackets should have two buoyancy compartments and comply with the regulations for fixed buoyancy type lifejackets. They should:

- Inflate automatically on immersion and be capable of manual inflation by the mouth
- in the event of loss of buoyancy in one compartment, still meet the requirements for the standards required for lifejackets.

3.97 The self igniting light should last at least 2 hours.

3.98 Emit smoke of a highly visible colour at a uniform rate for a period of at least 15 minutes when floating in calm water and:

- Not ignite explosively or emit any flame during the entire smoke emission of the signal
- not be swamped in a seaway
- continue to emit smoke when swamped in a seaway for a period of at least 10 seconds
- be capable of withstanding the drop test into the water from the stowed position or from 30 metres, whichever is greater.

3.99 The muster list should be posted in:

- The bridge
- the engine room
- the accommodation.

3.100 Only one type of release mechanism is permitted.

3.101 As long as necessary to reach the waterline in the lightest sea-going draught.

3.102 Approximately 4 metres longer than the hawser on the sea anchor.

3.103 These are only to be used for securing to a liferaft, lifeboat or person in the water, not for securing the EPIRB to the railing.

3.104 Each crew member to participate in one abandon ship and one fire drill per month.

3.105 The general emergency signal consists of seven or more short blasts followed by one long blast on the ship's whistle.

3.106 When 25% of the crew members have not participated in a drill onboard that ship in the previous month.

3.107 All lifeboats and other LSA are required to be checked against a checklist.

3.108 Lifeboat water spray systems are required to be tested monthly and flushed through with fresh-water.

3.109 It is only designed to hoist the lifeboat and its handling crew, not with a full load.

3.110 Totally Enclosed Motor Propelled Survival Craft.

3.111 Put on warm clothing and a lifejacket and proceed to the muster station.

3.112 There are 2 heaving lines in a lifeboat.

3.113 A ladder is provided which should be attached to the gunwale.

3.114 On a waterproof rescue signal card in the survival craft lockers.

3.115 Lifeboats are provided with:

- 2 x portable dry powder extinguisher
- bucket of sand
- an abundant supply of seawater.

3.116 On the pyrotechnics themselves.

3.117 The order to abandon ship is only given by word of mouth.

3.118 Tricing penants are for taking the boat in close to the embarkation deck.

3.119 The list limits are 25 degrees.

3.120 Skids protect the boat from damage during launch, against a list down the ship's side.

3.121 Position davit over the liferaft and connect to the liferaft container.

- Holding on to the bowsing-in lines, swing the raft outboard
- inflate raft
- make fast bowsing-in lines
- board the liferaft
- release bowsing-in lines
- pull on the lowering wire
- when waterbourne pull the toggle to release raft from the block
- paddle away.

3.122 To board the liferaft:

- Check that the painter is fast
- remove the guard rail
- kick over the boarding ladder
- release container lashing (senhouse slip)
- throw raft overside
- pull painter and inflate
- pull raft into bottom of ladder and board
- cut painter and paddle away.

3.123 There is no painter on a davit-launched liferaft.

3.124 6 liferafts and 150 persons.

3.125 Approach from the leeward side of the liferaft, grab the righting strop and with feet on becketed line. Pull until you can put your feet on the CO_2 cylinder then pull until raft falls clear.

3.126 Paddle to within 15 feet of them then throw the heaving quoit.

3.127 Drift is reduced by the sea anchor and the pockets underneath.

3.128 Embarkation ladders are required for lifeboats launched down the side of the ship. However, they are not required to be provided at the stern for free-fall lifeboats.

3.129 Bowsing-in tapes.

3.130 The minimum weight of wearer, 'Front', the manufacturer's name and date of survey are all marked on a lifejacket.

3.131 In addition to a lifejacket being carried for every person onboard:

- For passenger ships on voyages greater than 24 hours infant lifejacket equal to 2.5% of the number of passengers onboard
- for passenger ships on voyages less than 24 hours a lifejacket for each infant onboard

- childrens lifejackets equal to 10% of the number of passengers onboard, or a number equal to the number of children if more than 10% are onboard
- a sufficient number of extra lifejackets for watchkeepers, etc
- a sufficient number of accessories to be available if lifejackets are not designed for persons up to 140 kg and 1750 mm chest girth
- in addition to that above, passenger ships are to carry an additional 5% of the total number of persons onboard, stowed in conspicuous places and/or muster stations.

3.132 The valves are intended to allow air out of the legs.

3.133 TPA is a large bag that will protect the wearer from the wind and spray and retain heat inside. It is of assistance to help warm someone up who may have become hypothermic as another person may fit inside, if necessary to share body heat and raise the hypothermic parsons temperature.

3.134 No, it will float with its gunwale clear of the water, even when fully laden with full complement. This is due to the inherent buoyancy normally under the side benches.

3.135 Brightly coloured jacket, retro reflective tape, a whistle and a light (lasting at least 8 hours) are on a lifejacket.

3.136 Five lights in total:
- Searchlight
- navigation light
- lamp or internal lighting
- signalling torch
- compass light.

3.137 A sea anchor comprises:
- A tapered canvas bag
- the bridle

- the hawser (securing line)
- the tripping line.

3.138 On the liferaft submerging 4 metres, the hydrostatic release unit (HRU) activates, allowing the liferaft cannister to float to the surface. At this time the painter is still secured to the ship and is pulled out of the cannister as the ship continues to sink, when the ship has sunk about 25 metres it will tighten and inflate the raft. As the ship continues to sink and tries to pull the liferaft under, the strain on the weak-link will cause it to break and the raft will float free.

3.139 Initial actions after launching a liferaft are:

- Cut the painter and get clear
- stream the drogue/sea anchor
- close down the doors
- maintain the raft.

3.140 There is no difference in the pyrotechnics carried in a lifeboat and that carried in a liferaft.

3.141 A repair kit consists of cone shaped leak stoppers, patches and adhesive, valve stoppers and possibly clamps.

3.142 The casualty should be turned back to the raft and lifted under the arms.

3.143 By deflating the floor and throwing water over the raft.

3.144 Body heat of occupants should warm up the raft when the doors are closed. Dry off your clothing, use TPAs and gentle exercise can help.

3.145 One float free EPIRB is required as the minimum, ie a 406 MHz EPIRB.

3.146 There is normally an indicator light which will flash.

3.147 An EPIRB will normally transmit for 48 hours.

3.148 No, leave the EPIRB on until rescued.

3.149 A SART (Search and Rescue Transponder) is an electronic radar beacon which receives a radar signal from searching ship's radar signal, alters it and then re-transmits it.

3.150 A series of dots in a line and when within 1 nautical mile, a series of circles around the centre of the radar screen.

3.151 A SART will operate for 96 hours on stand-by and 8 hours when interrogated by a radar set.

3.152 Two, one for each lifeboat/survival craft normally kept one on each side of the bridge.

3.153 In addition to the rapid speed and clearance of launching, it can be launched with the ship listing up to 70 degrees.

3.154 On the ship's port quarter as the pilot and helicopter winch is on it's starboard side.

4 Checklists

4.1 Check and ensure that:

- Flags are available - country flag and additional flags are available as required for signalling
- course recorder - course readout verified and in correct quadrant, paper in machine sufficient for voyage. UTC reading confirmed and enter the date, time of checking and port name on paper
- engine movement recorder, compare reading when reducing from full sea speed to manouevering full, GMT/UTC readout confirmed, enter date and port name on paper
- clocks are synchronised
- internal communications equipment in operation
- signalling lamps are working
- deck lighting is operational
- provision for extra lookouts are made as required for periods of hand steering
- hand steering tested
- the engine room is notified of deck power requirements
- crew advised of time of stand-by
- note made of required VHF Channels
- radio check of VHF unit and hand-held units to be used for mooring operations
- update ETA in accordance with local regulations and details of any dangerous/hazardous goods
- notice as required for the engine room
- ensure anchors are cleared in ample time.

4.2 Consider the following when preparing the 'In-Port Passage Plan':

- Available port information from port handbooks, sailing directions, the 'Guide to Port Entry', company directives or past experience
- tide and current data for the port and approaches

- under keel clearance in port approaches and at the berth
- present draught fore and aft available on the bridge
- latest weather report received
- all relevant charts and publications are corrected and up-to-date
- courses are laid off on charts, passage plan produced and agreed by the Master
- the Master/Pilot exchange form completed.

4.3 The following should be read:

- Master's and Company's Standing Orders
- supplementary Master's instructions or Night Orders
- navigational warnings
- weather forecast.

The following information should be among that passed on:

- Position plotted on chart and the methods being used to obtain
- course and any allowances for set, drift and leeway
- speed
- tidal conditions, currents experienced or anticipated
- weather and visibility
- operational condition of navigational equipment
- gyro/magnetic compass errors
- gyro repeaters compared with master gyro compass during the handover
- movement of ships within sight or within area
- correct identification of navigational lights
- conditions likely to be encountered on watch
- condition of engine room, manned/unmanned and the duty engineer
- hydrodynamic effects on the UKC-heel, trim, squat, etc
- if in open water, the location and means of contacting lookout/ helmsman

- any personnel involved in entry to enclosed space/hold space and log kept
- any particular VHF station that the ship is listening to.

4.4 Refer to the 'ICS Guide to Helicopter/Ship Operations'.

Checks would include:

- All loose objects within and adjacent to the operating area, secured or removed
- all aerials, standing or running gear above and in the vicinity of the operating area, lowered or secured
- has a pennant or windsock been hoisted where it can clearly be seen by the helicopter pilot? In the abscence of a windsock the 'Code Flag and Answering Pennant' is commonly hoisted.
- leader of the deck party to have a radio for communications with the bridge
- fire hoses ready
- foam hoses/monitors and portable foam equipment to be ready
- foam station/room manned and in radio contact
- extinguishers ready - 2 × 45 kg Dry Powder, 1 × 18 kg CO_2
- deck party prepared 4 persons wearing fire protective suits
- rescue party detailed
- rescue boat ready for lowering
- following equipment to hand:
    - large axe
    - crowbar
    - wire cutters
    - red emergency signalling torch (flashing red indicates operations finished
- marshalling batons at night
- correct navigation lights exhibited - 'restricted in her ability to manouevre'

- the hook handler to be equipped with a helmet, strong rubber gloves and rubber soled shoes to avoid the danger of static discharge
- the landing area must be clear
- the operating area must be free of heavy spray and seas on deck
- side rails and, where necessary, awnings, stanchions and other obstructions must be lowered or removed
- portable pipes to be removed and the remaining apex ends blanked off
- all personnel to be warned to keep clear of rotors and exhausts.

4.5 The following should be checked/completed before departure:

- Secure the vessel for sea
- stowaway checks made and unauthorised personnel searched for
- deck lighting should be adequate for operations
- crew ready at stations
- anchors ready as required
- harbour pins removed from lifeboat davits
- all crew confirmed onboard
- power available on deck.

4.6 The following should be checked/completed before departure:

- Bridge movement book, port of departure and date entered
- course recorder checked
- engine movement recorder checked
- engine Room notified of deck power requirements
- departure draught noted on Master/Pilot exchange form and other relevant forms
- echo sounder
- gyro compass and repeaters
- magnetic compass
- pilot embarking/disembarking arrangements

- radar/ARPA
- speed/distance recorder 'zeroed' prior to departure and again at FAOP, the intermediate distance noted as harbour steaming
- bridge/engine room telegraph
- communications, internal and external
- navigation lights/shapes including emergency navigation lights/shapes for NUC and at anchor
- ship's whistles
- signalling lamps
- steering gear tested with 2 motors running while manoeuvring
- clocks synchronised.

4.7 The following should be ready:

- Passage plan prepared for intended voyage
- charts for the intended voyage and other up-to-date nautical publications
- ECDIS/electronic charts should be prepared
- courses laid off on charts
- master/pilot exchange form completed
- GPS set up, ensuring on correct geodetic data, ie WGS 72 or 84
- navigational warnings received and charts updated
- weather forecast received
- navtex prepared.

4.8 At least 12 hours before departure from port, the steering gear should be tested in accordance with SOLAS Chapter V Reg 19.2, and should include checks where applicable of the following:

- Main steering gear
- auxiliary steering gear
- all remote steering gear systems
- steering position on the navigating bridge
- emergency power supply
- rudder angle indicators in relation to actual position of rudder
- remote steering gear control system power failure alarms

- steering gear power unit failure alarms
- automatic isolating arrangements and other automatic equipment.

The test should include:

- Full rudder movement according to the required capabilities of the steering gear (recording results of hard over/hard over in seconds on the master/pilot card)
- visual inspection of the steering gear and its connecting linkage
- operation of the communications between the navigating bridge and the steering gear compartment.

4.9 Check and ensure the following:

- Distress message re-transmitted relayed
- continuous listening watch on all distress frequencies maintained
- merchant Ship Search and Rescue Manual (MERSAR) consulted
- communication established between surface units and SAR aircraft on air band radio and/or VHF channel 16
- positions, courses and speeds of other assisting units plotted
- radar made available for locating survival craft transponder (SART)
- a comprehensive log of events is maintained
- muster the required emergency parties as appropriate - rescue boat, first aid, etc.

4.10 The following actions should be carried out quickly:

- Lifebuoy with light, flare or smoke signal released
- avoiding action taken
- position of lifebuoy as search datum noted/press MOB button on any electronic positioning equipment
- 3 long blasts sounded and repeated as necessary.
- master informed
- engine room informed
- lookouts posted to keep person in sight

- ship manoeuvred to recover person as recommended
- rescue boat's crew assembled
- man-overboard warning broadcast
- after the event, inform DPA and MAIB or other relevant parties.

4.11 The following actions should be taken in the event of fire:

- Emergency alarm sounded, muster completed, POB accounted for
- all concerned notified of seat of fire
- ventilation fans off
- automatic fire doors, watertight doors closed, or as per action plan
- fire pump started
- deck lighting switched on
- vessel's position available satellite terminal and other automatic distress transmitters, updated as necessary
- update AIS status.

4.12 In the event of stranding the following actions are required:

- Engines stopped
- emergency alarm sounded
- watertight doors closed
- VHF watch maintained on channel 16
- broadcast made to other ships
- sound signals made
- lights/shapes exhibited
- deck lighting switched on
- damage assessment
- bilges and tanks sounded
- overside soundings taken
- vessels position available, satellite terminal and other automatic distress transmitters updated as necessary
- monitor weather and tidal conditions
- inform DPA and MAIB or other relevant parties
- update AIS status.

4.13 In the event of imminent collision

- Sound the emergency alarm
- ship manoeuvred to minimise effects of collision
- watertight doors and automatic fire doors closed
- deck lighting switched on
- VHF kept on channel 16 and, if appropriate, channel 13
- passengers and crew mustered at emergency stations
- vessel's position available, satellite terminal and other automatic distress transmitters updated as necessary
- exhibit appropriate lights and shapes
- bilges and tanks sounded after collision
- checks made for fire/damage assessment
- if vessels have become stuck together, do not try to 'manoeuvre out' until a full damage assessment of both vessels has been made
- update AIS status.

4.14 In the event of bridge control telegraph failure:

- Switch to engine room control
- duty engineer/engine room informed
- emergency communications established with engine room
- informed the Master.

4.15 In the event of gyrofailure:

- Magnetic compass or any alternative means used for the heading
- inform the Master
- person responsible for the gyro maintenance should be informed
- engine room informed
- effect of failure on other navigational aids considered.

4.16 In the event of steering failure:

- Engine room informed and alternative/emergency steering engaged
- Master to be informed

- 'Not Under Command' shapes or lights exhibited
- appropriate sound signal made
- if necessary, take way of the ship
- consider anchoring
- broadcast warning to other vessels
- update AIS status.

4.17 In the event of main engine failure:

- Inform Master
- close watertight doors
- rudder and thrusters used to best navigational advantage
- preparations made for anchoring if in shallow water
- 'Not Under Command' shapes or lights exhibited
- warning broadcast
- update AIS Status
- monitor weather and tidal conditions.

4.18 The following should be prepared/checked:

- Advise the following
  - Master
  - engine room
  - crew
- watertight doors shut as appropriate
- speed adjusted
- searchlights rigged
- monitoring ice advisory service broadcasts
- transmit danger message in accordance with SOLAS Chapter V Reg 2(a).

4.19 In restricted visibility the following should be done:

- Master and engine room informed
- following equipment brought in to operation:
  - radar/ARPA
  - manual Steering
  - VHF
  - fog signalling apparatus

  - navigation lights
  - echo sounder
  - watertight doors
- additional lookouts posted
- engines ready for immediate manoeuvre (SBE)
- if the ship's position is in doubt consider anchoring.

4.20 Prior to anchoring:

- Anchor plan to be prepared, taking into account:
  - speed reduction in ample time and the engine tested astern
  - direction/strength of wind/current
  - tidal stream when manouevring at low speeds
  - need for adequate searoom particularly to seaward
  - abort plan
- inform the following of the time of 'stand-by':
  - the Master
  - the engine room
  - the anchor party
- the following equipment to be ready for use:
  - anchors
  - lights/shapes
  - sound signalling equipment
- vessel's position noted on dropping anchor. Ship's heading noted to determine the exact position where the anchor was dropped and prepare the swinging circle on chart.

4.21 The following should be considered when planning a coastal passage or a passage through a TSS:

- Charts and publications to be used corrected and up-to-date
- the following factors must be taken into consideration when planning the passage:
  - advice/recommendation in sailing directions
  - ship's draught
  - under keel clearance
  - effect of squat on under keel clearance in shallow water

  - tides and currents
  - weather, particularly in areas renowned for poor visibility
  - available navigational aids and their accuracy
  - position-fixing methods to be used
  - daylight/night-time passing of danger points
  - traffic likely to be encountered - flow type and volume
  - any requirements for traffic separation/routing schemes
- full consideration given the collision regulations
- local/coastal warning broadcasts to be monitored
- participation in area reporting system, ie MAREP
- courses laid off well clear of obstructions
- ship's position fixed at regular intervals and position checked by other means
- errors of gyro/magnetic compasses checked regularly and after each large alteration of course.

4.22 Consider the following:

- All charts and nautical publications to be used corrected and up-to-date
- a comprehensive passage plan for the voyage should have been prepared
- navarea warning broadcasts to be monitored
- the vessel participating in a vessel reporting system such as AMVER
- the ship's position is to be fixed at regular intervals
- error of Gyro/Magnetic Compass to be determined at least once a watch
- weather conditions and forecasts are to be monitored.

4.23 Check the following

- The following to be advised of ETA/ETD:
  - the Master
  - the engine room
  - the pilot station
- determine which side the Pilot will embark/disembark

- complete the Pilot information card
- the engine room to be advised of the time of 'stand-by'
- the Pilot embarkation/disembarkation arrangements to be checked ready for use
- a deck officer is to be nominated to meet the Pilot and conduct him to/from the bridge
- the Pilot is to be shown the lifesaving equipment that is available for his use.

4.24 Test the following:

- Bridge and engine room telegraphs
- revolution indicators and check with Engine Room as to what they are delivering
- bridge telephones
- clocks and chronometers
- general emergency alarm bell
- ship's whistle (but not in poor visibility, or when other vessels are near)
- steering gear motors changed over.

4.25 Prior to heavy weather check the following:

- The following have been informed:
    - the Master
    - the engine room
    - the crew
- have all moveable objects been secured, on deck, below deck, ports and deadlights
- speed and course adjusted as necessary
- are hull openings and watertight doors secured
- a helmsman and lookout should be posted
- crew warned to avoid upper deck areas made dangerous by the weather
- safety lines and hand ropes rigged as neccessary
- instructions have been issued on the following matters:
    - monitoring weather reports & increase frequency

  - transmitting weather reports to the appropriate authorities or in the case of a tropical revolving storm, transmit danger message in accordance with SOLAS 1974 Chapter V Reg 2(a).

4.26 You would advise the following:

- The depth of water at the berth
- the ship's draught
- the time of high and low waters and the height
- mooring arrangements
- state of main engines and availability for use
- all work being carried onboard the ship
- quantity of cargo onboard, amounts to be loaded or unloaded
- amount of ballast remaining
- signals being exhibited
- number of crew ashore, presence of shore personnel onboard
- readiness of fire fighting equipment
- any special port regulations including security requirements
- masters orders and Chief Officers orders
- communication between vessel and shore and means of raising assistance in an emergency
- any other circumstances, including weather conditions, important to the safety of the ship.

4.27 During cargo watch the duty officer should:

- Make rounds to inspect the ship regularly paying attention to:
  - the gangway
  - moorings, particularly at the turn of the tide or berths with a large rise and fall of tide
  - draught
  - under keel clearance
  - avoid dangerous listing or trim during cargo operations
  - state of the weather
  - observance of safety and fire prevention regulations
  - water levels in bilges, such as a pump room or void space

    - personnel onboard and their locations
    - lights or signals exhibited
- ensure the fire plan is fully updated
- monitor work being undertaken including any permits to work in use
- on receiving warning of bad weather, take necessary steps to protect the ship personnel and cargo
- ensure every precaution is taken to prevent pollution by your ship
- in the event of an emergency threatening the safety of the ship, raise the alarm, inform the Master of the situation and take all possible measures to prevent any damage to the ship. If necessary, request assistance from shore authorities or other vessels
- be aware of the state of the vessel's stability
- take necessary actions to prevent accidents or damage when propellers are to be turned
- enter in the appropriate log book all important events affecting the ship.

4.28 When taking the watch in port you should check:

- The moorings
- that the appropriate signals are hoisted and exhibited
- all safety measures and fire protection regulations are being observed
- that all cargo, especially hazardous cargo, being loaded or discharged and actions to be taken in the event of spillage or fire are clear and understood
- that means of access are clear are correctly set up
- the depth of water and vessels draught
- any work being undertaken onboard and that permits to work are in force
- the number of crew onboard
- any special port requirements and regulations
- Master's Standing Orders.

4.29 It is important to study the operation of the following equipment:

- Alarms
- bridge/chart room lighting and the operation of deck and overside lighting
- communications, internal and external
- direction finder (if fitted)
- echo sounder, including location of any remote layouts
- electronic navigational position fixing aids
- emergency arrangements in the event of mains power failure
- hazard monitoring equipment
- gyro compass and repeaters
- magnetic compass
- navigation lights, including emergency navigation, not under command, aldis lamp and any other signal lights
- radar and associated plotting aids
- safety equipment such as pyrotechnics
- speed/distance recorder
- steering gear, including manual, auto-pilot and emergency changeover arrangements
- telegraph, including control of main engines and change-over procedures
- control of watertight doors
- determine the location and operation of ancilliary bridge equipment including binoculars, signalling flags, meteorological equipment
- stowage of chart and hydrographic publications
- read the Master's Standing orders
- electronic chart system and operation.

5 Bridge Instruments

5.1 The following information is recorded on the VDR:

- Date and time
- ship's position
- ship's speed
- heading
- bridge audio
- radar data, post-display selection
- echo sounder, depth beneath the keel
- rudder order and response
- hull openings (doors) status
- watertight and fire door status
- accelerations, hull stresses (if the ship is fitted with a monitoring system)
- wind speed and wind direction.(if ship fitted with sensors)
- all IMO mandatory alarms status.

5.2 There are three basic functional parts of a shipboard VDR system. They are:

1. Sensor interfaces that accept signals from the various shipboard systems and convert the data into a format that can be recorded by the VDR
2. a data acquisition and recording module, which receives, processes and stores data from the interface
3. the protective memory capsule, which contains the final recording medium.

In addition, the VDR system will include a power supply and dedicated reserve power source that must operate continuously for at least two hours following a mains power failure.

5.3 Two types of data capsule are permitted under the IEC 61996 specification: float free and submersible.

- A float free device must automatically detach itself from a sinking ship. It must be equipped with a flashing light and

transmit a radio homing signal with a battery life of at least 7 days
- a submersible data capsule must be equipped with an acoustic underwater beacon with a battery life of at least 30 days
- a means must be provided for retrieving stored information via an external device without opening the protective capsule
- recording must be continuous and automatic. All stored data items must be retained at least 12 hours.

5.4 The system coverage range is similar to other VHF applications, essentially depending on the height of the antenna. Its propagation is slightly better than that of radar, due to the longer wavelength, so it's possible to 'see' around bends and behind islands if the land masses are not too high.

A typical value to be expected at sea is nominally 20 nautical miles.

With the help of repeater stations, the coverage for both ship and VTS stations can be improved considerably.

5.5 A Class A AIS unit broadcasts the following information every 2 to 10 seconds while underway, and every 3 minutes while at anchor:
- MMSI number
- navigation status - 'at anchor', 'under way using engine', 'not under command', etc
- rate of turn - right or left
- speed over ground
- position accuracy - differential GPS
- longitude and Latitude
- course over ground - relative to true north
- true heading
- time stamp - The universal time to nearest second.

In addition, the Class A AIS unit broadcasts the following information every 6 minutes:
- MMSI number
- IMO number

- radio call sign
- name of ship
- type of ship/cargo
- dimensions of ship
- location on ship where reference point for position reports is located
- type of position fixing device
- draught of ship
- destination
- estimated time of arrival at destination.

5.6 There are five major areas where AIS improves radar:

- It helps radar find targets around a cape, behind islands and around bends as long as the land masses are not too high
- it translates radar echoes into ship names, which is useful for communications
- it improves prediction of a target's path by taking into account its rate of turn (ROT)
- it extends beyond radar's range
- it helps to clarify a target's intentions, as it can display target destinations, draught, size and navigation status.

5.7 Connecting AIS to radar can complicate matters:

- An AIS target's GPS information may, for various reasons, be inaccurate and should be compared with radar
- a target's AIS position may be different from the position of its echo on the radar screen
- ROT-corrected (T)CPA calculations are complex, dynamic and may differ from radar.

5.8 An Electronic Chart Information and Display System (ECDIS) is, a navigation information system that complies with regulation V/20 of the 1974 SOLAS Convention for chart requirements, so long as it is adequately backed up with other arrangements.

ECDIS systems are a legal equivalent to paper charts only if meeting the Performance Standards of the IHO (International Hydrographic Organization).

An Electronic Charting System (ECS) is any other system that displays electronic chart information for navigation but does not meet the requirements of an ECDIS system. It is not the legal equivalent of a paper chart and may only be used for "situational awareness." An ECS *may* be used as a back up for an ECDIS system.

5.9 Raster charts: raster charts are scanned paper charts. The charts are scanned into a bitmap image.

IMO resolution MSC.232(82) permits ECDIS equipment to operate in a Raster Chart Display System (RCDS) mode in the absence of ENC vector charts, but an appropriate paper chart folio must be carried.

Vector charts: vector charts consist of a database of objects made up of points and lines (vectors) with associated attributes (like latitude, longitude, height, characteristics).

ENCs (Electronic Navigational Charts) are vector charts that conform to IHO specifications, as contained in IHO Publication S-57.

5.10 The advantages of raster charts are:

- They look just like a paper chart, so are familiar to seafarers
- they are comparatively inexpensive and easy to produce
- they run easily on a PC
- they currently have world-wide availability.

The disadvantages of raster charts are:

- Individual elements of the file are difficult to change
- less versatile than vector charts
- data files can be very large, depending on the resolution.

5.11 The advantages of vector charts are:

- Smaller file sizes but can display much more detail than a raster chart
- the data is organized in layers, each with discreet features, giving the user control over what level and type of detail they want to display
- the database can be accessed quickly by clicking a symbol for more information. For example, the user can click on a light and a box will appear that contains all the information on the light
- vector charts can be linked to other onboard systems to provide automatic features such as warning alarms to check a ship's position along the ship's intended track.

The main disadvantages of vector charts is coverage, which currently is restricted to a small number of areas, and the additional training required to fully understand the systems.

5.12

- Automatic positioning is usually accomplished by GPS. With the selective availability disabled since 1st May 2000, GPS is now accurate to 20 to 30 metres for however, the GPS accuracy could be degraded if the selective availability is switched on again
- like any other piece of equipment, ECDIS may malfunction. To be certified, any ECDIS system must have adequate back up. A means to check the operation of ECDIS must be in place, which may include positioning info using visual bearings, radar ranges and celestial observations
- electronic charts may have embedded errors. Raster and vector charts retain the inaccuracies and incongruities of the source from which they are derived. These charts may be based on old survey data
- human error, primarily due to a lack of understanding of the system used onboard, can have serious consequences.

5.13 An Integrated Bridge System consists of the following components:

1. Electronic Chart Display and Information System (ECDIS).
2. System Display: a unit that displays an electronic chart with the ship's position on it. It also provides information on sensor status, navigation information, collision avoidance information as well as own ship control systems information.
3. Planning Station: a computer station that interfaces with the user. This is where all navigation information is input.
4. Control Systems: a system that is capable of maintaining a track automatically.
5. Sensor Inputs: inputs from the radar and ARPA, echosounder, GPS, LORAN, gyrocompass and other sensors to provide position data and overlays. Provides a capability of producing an integrated display, showing all contacts and navigation hazards on one screen.
6. Computer Processors and Networks: the hardware needed to process the sensor information as well as the flow of information to each subsystem component.

5.14
- The display indicates the real time position
- the plotting is done automatically
- human error in navigation is minimised
- provides an alert system to navigation dangers
- increases awareness in low visibility.

6 Security

6.1

1. To establish co-operation between contracting governments, government agencies, local authorities and the shipping/port industries to detect security threats and take preventative measures against security incidents affecting ships or port facilities used in international trade.
2. To establish the respective roles and responsibilities of the contracting governments, government agencies, local administrations and the shipping and port industries, at a national and international level, for ensuring maritime security.
3. To ensure the early and efficient collection and exchange of security-related information.
4. To provide a methodology for security assessments so as to have in place plans and procedures to react to changing security levels.
5. To ensure confidence that adequate and proportionate maritime security measures are in place.

6.2 A Ship Security Plan (SSP) is a plan developed to ensure the application of measures onboard the ship, which are designed to protect persons onboard, cargo, cargo transport units, ship's stores or the ship from the risks of a security incident.

6.3 Security level 1 the 'normal' level for which minimum appropriate protective security measures shall be maintained at all times.

Security level 2 the 'heightened' level for which appropriate additional protective security measures shall be maintained for a period of time as a result of heightened risk of a security incident.

Security level 3 the 'exceptional' level for which further specific protective security measures shall be maintained for a limited period of time when a security incident is probable or imminent, although it may not be possible to identify the specific target.

6.4 The following types of vessels, engaged on international voyages:

- Passenger ships, including high-speed passenger craft
- cargo ships, including high-speed craft, of 500 gross tonnage and upwards
- mobile offshore drilling units.

6.5 Ports which serve ships that the ISPS Code applies to and are are engaged on international voyages.

6.6

- Ensuring the performance of all ship security duties
- controlling access to the ship
- controlling the embarkation of persons and their effects
- monitoring restricted areas to ensure that only authorised persons have access
- monitoring of deck areas and areas surrounding the ship
- supervising the handling of cargo and ship's stores
- ensuring that security communication is readily available.

6.7 At security level 2, the additional security measures specified in the SSP shall be implemented, taking into account the guidance given in part B of the ISPS Code.

6.8 At security level 3, the additional security measures specified in the SSP shall be implemented, taking into account the guidance given in part B of the ISPS Code.

6.9 It should comprise of at least the following elements:

- Identification of existing security measures, procedures and operations
- identification and evaluation of key shipboard operations that are important to protect
- identification of possible threats to the key shipboard operations and the likelihood of their occurrence, in order to establish and prioritise security measures
- identification of weaknesses, including human factors, in the infrastructure, policies and procedures.

6.10 It should be accompanied by the security assessment on the basis of which the plan or the amendments have been developed.

6.11 The SSP should address:

- Measures designed to prevent weapons, dangerous substances and devices intended for use against persons, ships or ports and the carriage of which is not authorised from being taken onboard the ship
- identification of the restricted areas and measures for the prevention of unauthorised access to them
- measures for the prevention of unauthorised access to this ship
- procedures for responding to security threats or breaches of security, including provisions for maintaining critical operations of the ship or ship/port interface
- procedures for responding to any security instructions contracting governments may give a security level 3
- procedures for evacuation in case of security threats or breaches of security
- duties of shipboard personnel assigned security responsibilities and of other shipboard personnel on security aspects
- procedures for auditing the security activities
- procedures for training, drills and exercises associated with the plan
- procedures for interfacing with port facility security activities
- procedures for the periodic review of the plan and for updating
- procedures for reporting security incidents
- identification of the Ship Security Officer (SSO)
- identification of the Company Security Officer (CSO), including 24-hour contact details
- procedures to ensure the inspection, testing, calibration and maintenance of any security equipment provided onboard
- frequency for testing or calibration of any security equipment provided onboard

- identification of the locations where the ship security alert system activation points are provided
- procedures, instructions and guidance on the use of the ship security alert system, including the testing, activation, deactivation and resetting and to limit false alerts.

6.12 Records of the following activities should be retained onboard.

- Training, drills and exercises
- security threats and security incidents
- breaches of security
- changes in security level
- communications relating to the direct security of the ship such as specific threats to the ship or to port facilities the ship is, or has been, in
- internal audits and reviews of security activities
- periodic review of the ship security assessment
- periodic review of the Ship Security Plan
- implementation of any amendments to the plan
- maintenance, calibration and testing of any security equipment provided onboard, including testing of the ship security alert system.

6.13 The duties of the SSO shall include, but are not limited to:

- Undertaking regular security inspections of the ship to ensure that appropriate security measures are maintained
- maintaining and supervising the implementation of the SSP, including any amendments to the plan
- co-ordinating the security aspects of the handling of cargo and ship's stores with other shipboard personnel and with the relevant Port Facility Security Officers (PFSO)
- proposing modifications to the SSP
- reporting to the CSO any deficiencies and non-conformities identified during internal audits, periodic reviews, security inspections and verification of compliance and implementing any corrective actions.

- enhancing security awareness and vigilance onboard
- ensuring that adequate training has been provided to shipboard personnel, as appropriate
- reporting all security incidents
- co-ordinating implementation of the SSP with the CSO and the relevant PFSO
- ensuring that security equipment is properly operated, tested, calibrated and maintained.

6.14 A port facility is required to act upon the security levels set by the contracting government within whose territory it is located.

6.15 At security level 1, the following activities shall be carried out through appropriate measures in all port facilities:

- Ensure that all port facility security duties are performed
- controlling access to the port facility
- monitoring of the port facility, including anchoring and berthing areas
- monitoring restricted areas to ensure that only authorised persons have access
- supervising the handling of cargo
- supervising the handling of ship's stores
- ensuring that security communication is readily available.

6.16 An initial survey before the ISPS certificate is issued for the first time shall include a complete verification of its security system, any associated security equipment covered by the relevant provisions of the ISPS Code and of the approved ship security plan.

This verification shall ensure that the security system and any associated security equipment of the ship fully complies with the applicable requirements of the ISPS Code, is in satisfactory condition and fit for the service for which the ship is intended.

For a ship that the ISPS applies to, what should the renewal survey of the ISPS certificate consist of and at what intervals?

A renewal survey of the ISPS certificate is at intervals specified by the Administration, but not exceeding five years.

This verification shall ensure that the security system and any associated security equipment of the ship fully complies with the applicable requirements of the ISPS Code and the approved SSP, is in satisfactory condition and fit for the service that the ship is intended for.

6.17 There should be at least one intermediate survey. If only one intermediate survey is carried out it shall take place between the second and third anniversary date of the certificate.

6.18 The intermediate survey should include the inspection of the security system and any associated security equipment, of the ship to ensure that it remains satisfactory for the service for which the ship is intended.

6.19 An International Ship Security Certificate (ISSC) is valid for a period specified by the Administration, but it shall not exceed five years.

6.20 It can apply to ships and port facilities.

6.21 Setting security level 3 should be an exceptional measure applying only when there is credible information that a security incident is probable or imminent.

6.22 Administrations may wish to use NAVTEX messages or Notices to Mariners as the method for notifying such changes in security levels to the ship, the CSO and SSO. Or, they may wish to consider other methods of communication that provide equivalent or better speed and coverage.

6.23 The following information may be required:

- Confirmation of any special or additional measures taken by the ship during its last 10 calls at a port facility
- any Declarations of Security that were entered into with port facilities or other ships

- confirmation that appropriate ship security procedures were maintained during ship-to-ship activity conducted within the period of the last 10 calls at a port facility
- information contained in the Continuous Synopsis Record (CSR)
- location of the ship at the time the report is made
- expected time of arrival of the ship in port
- crew list
- general description of cargo aboard the ship
- passenger list
- information required to be carried under Chapter XI-2 of SOLAS.

6.24 A ship security assessment should address the following elements onboard or within the ship:

- Physical security
- structural integrity
- personnel protection systems
- procedural policies
- radio and telecommunication systems, including computer systems and networks
- other areas that may, if damaged or used for illicit observation, pose a risk to persons, property, or operations onboard the ship or within the port facility.

6.25 The information required to conduct an assessment by the CSO would include:

- The general layout of the ship
- the location of areas which should have restricted access, such as navigation bridge, machinery spaces and other control stations
- the location and function of each actual or potential ship access point
- changes in the tide which may impact on the vulnerability or security of the ship

- the cargo spaces and stowage arrangements
- the locations where the ship's stores and essential maintenance equipment is stored
- the locations where unaccompanied baggage is stored
- the emergency and stand-by equipment available to maintain essential services
- the number of ship's personnel, any existing security duties and any existing training requirement practices of the company
- existing security and safety equipment for the protection of passengers and ship's personnel
- escape and evacuation routes and assembly stations which have to be maintained to ensure the orderly and safe emergency evacuation of the ship
- existing agreements with private security companies providing ship/water-side security services
- existing security measures and procedures in effect, including inspection and control procedures, identification systems, surveillance and monitoring equipment, personnel identification documents and communication, alarms, lighting, access control and other appropriate systems.

6.26 The following would be listed in the SSA as important to protect:

- The ship's personnel
- passengers, visitors, vendors, repair technicians, port facility personnel, etc
- the capacity to maintain safe navigation and emergency response
- the cargo, particularly dangerous goods or hazardous substances
- the ship's stores
- the ship security communication equipment and systems, if any
- the ship's security surveillance equipment and systems, if any.

6.27 The SSA should consider all possible threats, which may include the following types of security incidents:

- Damage to, or destruction of, the ship or of a port facility, potentially by explosive devices, arson, sabotage or vandalism
- hijacking or seizure of the ship or of persons onboard
- tampering with cargo, essential ship equipment or systems or ship's stores
- unauthorised access or use, including presence of stowaways
- smuggling weapons or equipment, including weapons of mass destruction
- use of the ship to carry those intending to cause a security incident and/or their equipment
- use of the actual ship as a weapon or a means to cause damage or destruction
- attacks from seaward whilst at berth or at anchor
- attacks while at sea.

6.28 All SSPs should:

- Detail the organisational structure of security for the ship
- detail the ship's relationships with the company, port facilities, other ships and relevant authorities with security responsibility
- detail the communication systems to allow effective continuous communication within the ship and between the ship and others, including port facilities
- detail the basic operational and physical security measures for security level 1 that will always be in place
- detail the additional security measures that will allow the ship to progress without delay to security level 2 and when necessary, to security level 3
- provide a regular review, or audit, of the SSP and its amendments in response to experience or changing circumstances
- detail reporting procedures to the appropriate contracting government's contact points.

6.29 The SSP should establish the security measures covering all means of access to the ship identified in the Ship Security Assessment (SSA). This should include any:

- Access ladders
- access gangways
- access ramps
- access doors, sidescuttles, windows and ports
- mooring lines and anchor chains
- cranes and hoisting gear.

6.30 The SSP should establish the following:

- checking the identity of all persons seeking to board the ship and confirming their reasons for doing so by checking joining instructions, passenger tickets, boarding passes, work orders, etc
- in liaison with the port facility, the ship should ensure that designated secure areas are established in which inspections and searching of persons, baggage-including carry-on items, personal effects, vehicles and their contents can take place
- in liaison with the port facility, the ship should ensure that vehicles destined to be loaded onboard car carriers, RoRo and other passenger ships are subjected to search prior to loading in accordance with the frequency required in the SSP
- segregating checked persons and their personal effects from unchecked persons and their personal effects
- segregating embarking from disembarking passengers
- identifying access points that should be secured or attended to prevent unauthorised access
- securing, by locking or other means, access to unattended spaces adjoining to areas to which passengers and visitors have access
- providing security briefings to all ship personnel on possible threats, the procedures for reporting suspicious persons, objects or activities and the need for vigilance.

6.31 These could include:

- Assigning additional personnel to patrol deck areas during silent hours to deter unauthorised access
- limiting the number of access points to the ship, identifying those to be closed and the means of adequately securing them
- deterring waterside access to the ship including, for example, in liaison with the port facility, provision of boat patrols
- establishing a restricted area on the shore side of the ship, in close co-operation with the port facility
- increasing the frequency and detail of searches of persons, personal effects and vehicles being embarked or loaded onto the ship
- providing additional specific security briefings to all ship personnel on any identified threats, re-emphasising the procedures for reporting suspicious persons, objects, or activities and stressing the need for increased vigilance
- carrying out a full or partial search of the ship.

6.32 The ship should comply with the instructions issued by those responding to the security incident or threat thereof. The SSP should detail the security measures which could be taken by the ship, in close co-operation with those responding and the port facility, which may include:

- Limiting access to a single, controlled, access point
- granting access only to those responding to the security incident or threat thereof
- directing persons onboard
- suspension of embarkation or disembarkation
- suspension of cargo handling operations, deliveries, etc
- evacuation of the ship
- movement of the ship
- preparing for a full or partial search of the ship

6.33 Restricted areas may include:

- Navigation bridge, machinery spaces of category A and other control stations
- spaces containing security and surveillance equipment and systems and their controls and lighting system controls
- ventilation and air-conditioning systems and other similar spaces
- spaces with access to potable water tanks, pumps, or manifolds
- spaces containing dangerous goods or hazardous substances
- spaces containing cargo pumps and their controls
- cargo spaces and spaces containing ship's stores
- crew accommodation
- any other areas as determined by the CSO, through the SSA, to which access must be restricted to maintain the security of the ship.

6.34 The security measures relating to the delivery of ship's stores should:

- Ensure checking of ship's stores and package integrity
- prevent ship's stores from being accepted without inspection
- prevent tampering
- prevent ship's stores from being accepted unless ordered.

6.35 The ship should have the capability to monitor the ship, the restricted areas onboard and areas surrounding the ship. Such monitoring capabilities may include the use of:

- Lighting
- watchkeepers, security guards and deck watches, including patrols
- automatic intrusion-detection devices and surveillance equipment.

6.36 The SSO should have knowledge of, and receive training in, some or all of the following, as appropriate:

- Security administration

- relevant international conventions, codes and recommendations
- relevant government legislation and regulations
- responsibilities and functions of other security organisations
- methodology of ship security assessment
- methods of ship security surveys and inspections
- ship and port operations and conditions
- ship and port facility security measures
- emergency preparedness and response and contingency planning
- instruction techniques for security training and education, including security measures and procedures
- handling sensitive security-related information and security-related communications
- knowledge of current security threats and patterns
- recognition and detection of weapons, dangerous substances and devices
- recognition, on a non-discriminatory basis, of characteristics and behavioural patterns of persons who are likely to threaten security
- techniques used to circumvent security measures
- security equipment and systems and their operational limitations
- methods of conducting audits, inspections, control and monitoring
- methods of physical searches and non-intrusive inspections
- security drills and exercises, including drills and exercises with port facilities
- assessment of security drills and exercises.

6.37 The SSO should have adequate knowledge of, and receive training in, some or all of the following, as appropriate:

- The layout of the ship
- the SSP and related procedures (including scenario-based training on how to respond)

- operations of security equipment and systems
- testing, calibration and at-sea maintenance of security equipment and systems.

6.38 All shipboard personnel should have sufficient knowledge of and be familiar with relevant provisions of the SSP, including:

- The meaning and the consequential requirements of the different security levels
- knowledge of the emergency procedures and contingency plans
- recognition and detection of weapons, dangerous substances and devices
- recognition, on a non-discriminatory bases, of characteristics and behavioural patterns of persons who are likely to threaten security
- techniques used to circumvent security measures.

6.39 The objective of drills and exercises is to ensure that shipboard personnel are proficient in all assigned security duties at all security levels and the identification of any security-related deficiencies that need to be addressed.

6.40 To ensure the effective implementation of the provisions of the SSP, drills should be conducted at least once every three months.

In addition, in cases where more that 25% of the ship's personnel has been changed, at any one time, with personnel that has not previously participated in any drill on that ship within the last 3 months, a drill should be conducted within one week of the change.

6.41 These types of exercise, which may include participation of CSO, PFSO, relevant authorities of contracting governments as well as SSO, if available, should be carried out at least once each calendar year with no more than 18 months between the exercises. These exercises should test communications, co-ordination, resource availability and response.

6.42 These exercises may be:

- Full-scale or live
- tabletop simulation or seminar
- combined with other exercises held, such as search and rescue or emergency response exercises.

6.43 Restricted areas may include:

- Shore and water-side areas immediately adjacent to the ship
- embarkation and disembarkation areas, passenger and ship's personnel holding and processing areas, including search points
- areas where loading, unloading or storage of cargo and stores is undertaken
- locations where security-sensitive information, including cargo documentation, is held
- areas where dangerous goods and hazardous substances are held
- vessel traffic management system control rooms, aids to navigation and port control buildings, including security and surveillance control rooms
- areas where security and surveillance equipment are stored or located
- essential electrical, radio and telecommunications, water and other utility installations
- other locations in the port facility where access by vessels, vehicles and individuals should be restricted.

6.44 The Declaration of Security should cover the following activities:

- Ensuring the performance of all security duties
- monitoring restricted areas to ensure that only authorised personnel have access
- controlling access to the port facility
- controlling access to the ship
- monitoring of the port facility, including berthing areas surrounding the ship
- handling of cargo

- delivery of ship's stores
- handling unaccompanied baggage
- controlling the embarkation of persons and their effects
- ensuring that security communication is readily available between the ship and the port facility.

6.45 Prior to entering a port or whilst in a port within the territory of a contracting government, a ship shall comply with the requirements for the security level set by that contracting government where such security level is higher than the security level set by the Administration for that ship. You should contact the CSO.

6.46 The ship security alert system, when activated, shall:

- Initiate and transmit a ship-to-shore security alert to a competent authority designated by the administration, which in the circumstances may include the company, identifying the ship, its location and indicating that the security of the ship is under threat or has been compromised
- it should not send the ship security alert to any other ships
- it should not raise any alarm onboard the ship
- continue the ship security alert until deactivated and/or reset.

6.47 It should be capable of being activated from the navigation bridge and in at least one other location.

6.48 A contracting government may require that ships intending to enter its ports provide the following information:

- That the ship possesses a valid certificate and the name of its issuing authority
- the security level at which the ship is currently operating
- the security level at which the ship operated in any previous port where it has conducted a shop/port interface at the last 10 ports of call
- any special or additional security measures that were taken by the ship in any previous port where it has conducted a ship/port interface at the last 10 ports of call

- that the appropriate ship security procedures were maintained during any ship-to-ship activity at the last 10 ports of call
- any other practical security-related information, but not details of the SSP, taking into account the guidance given in part B of the ISPS Code.

6.49 The ship shall keep records of the information reported to the port in SOLAS XI-2 Regulation 9 for the last 10 calls at port facilities.

7 GMDSS

7.1 (a) 025856223

7.2 (d) Cancel the alert by notifying the appropriate MRCC/shore station.

7.3 (d) Perform 'Log-out' before switching off.

7.4 (a) VHF channel 70, 2187.5kHz, 8414.5kHz plus one other HF distress frequency.

7.5 (d) Cease transmission upon the first request of the coast station.

7.6 (a) Every day

7.7 (c) INMARSAT C

7.8 (a) 2182 kHz unless otherwise instructed.

7.9 (a) Public correspondence.

7.10 (d) Ship to aircraft engaged in SAR operations.

7.11 (d) ALRS Volume 5.

7.12 (c) Within range of a shore station having MF DSC.

7.13 (c) 2187.5 kHz plus channel 70.

7.14 (b) Through INMARSAT A.

7.15 (b) Allocates a free channel to be used for R/T over INMARSAT.

7.16 (c) A person nominated in Section B of the GMDSS radio log book.

7.17 (d) In Area A1 only.

7.18 (b) Medical Assistance.

7.19 (d) KKKK.

7.20 (c) 2187.5 kHz.

7.21 (d) ITU List of Coast Stations.

7.22 (c) 633500150.

7.23 The procedure is as follows:

- DSC distress alert - 8414.5 kHz
- all further traffic broadcast on 8291 kHz
- mayday (Repeated 3 times) this is Louames
- "mayday Louames MMYG2 232000123 53° 17'N 17° 43'W, vessel is taking in water and listing dangerously. Require immediate assistance. 23 persons onboard, abandoning to two lifeboats".
  SART and EPIRB devices to be activated.

7.24 The procedure is as follows:

- Log information
- watch on DSC Channel 70 and R/T Channel 16 and wait for CRS or MRCC to respond
- if, after a short interval, no response from CRS or MRCC
- acknowledge to vessel on R/T Channel 16
- relay, distress ashore
- CRS or MRCC will then be alerted and then will send a DSC acknowledgement to distress vessel.

7.25 The procedure is as follows:

- DSC safety alert - Channel 70
- (On Channel 16)
- 'securite' (3 times) all stations 'this is Louames'.
- 'securite surveying work involving a 1000 metre towed line will commence from the hours of 0600UTC and 2000UTC on the 20.06, in Latitudes 50° 05'N to 50° 15'N and Longitudes 002° 00'W to 002° 10'W. All vessels requested to keep at least 3 miles clear of area. DTG Louames MMYG2 232000123'.

7.26 The categories are:

(a) Distress alert or Urgency alert
(b) distress relay alert
(c) urgency alert
(d) safety alert.

7.27 Three methods:

(i) Quick send undesignated (ship's Inmarsat number and position)
(ii) designated distress (category of distress selected from a menu, plus above)
(iii) typed telex distress message (standard distress message).

7.28 The methods of distress are:

- VHF DSC & R/T alerting - Local ship-ship alerting
- MF DSC & R/T alerting - Local ship-ship alerting
- INMARSAT A, B or C alerting - Ship to shore alerting (Vessels under GMDSS are required to have a long distance method of communication either HF R/T and DSC or an INMARSAT facility.)
- EPIRB – (SARSAT COSPAS) Ship-shore
- INMARSAT E Ship-shore
- SART - Local ship - ship, ship - aircraft.

7.29 (a) The specific reasons are:

i That the Master feels that further assistance is required.
ii That the vessel in distress has not been able to transmit, your vessel transmits on its behalf.

(b) MF DSC distress RELAY on 2187.5 kHz. This message could contain such information as to the ID, position and category of the distress.
MF R/T Call and Message.
MaydayRelay (3 times) this is (Own ship's name).
MaydayRelay Name/Callsign/MMSI number.
Position and relevant message.

(c) MF and VHF DSC Distress Relays can be sent to 'All Stations' or an individual station.

An HF DSC Distress Relay should only be sent to an individual station.

7.30 (a) i. A SART (Search And Rescue Transponder) indicates both a distress situation and also the position of the SART device.

(a) ii. At a range of 5nm from a well mounted SART the display will indicate a line of 'blips' indicating bearing line to follow. The closest blip gives approximate range information.
Approaching 1nm the display will indicate the 'blips' increasing in width to form arcs, indicating the bearing line to follow. The closest arc gives approximate range information.
Within close range of the SART the arc increase to form complete circles. Bearing and range information is obscured.

(b) i. An EPIRB (Emergency Positioning Radio Beacon) indicates both a distress situation and also the position of the EPIRB device. Which should indicate the position of survivors.

(b) ii. SARSAT-COSPAS EPIRB (Worldwide coverage, operates on 406 MHz).
Inmarsat E EPIRB (Within the Inmarsat area A3, operates on 1.6 Ghz).
VHF DSC EPIRB (Used by A1 designated vessels only, operates on Channel 70).

7.31 (a) Used by vessel in distress or station designated to control the distress to impose radio silence after interference has been received from another station.

(b) Used by vessel in distress or station designated to control the distress to announce that the distress has been terminated. Allows vessels monitoring to stand down and for correct completion of the radio log.

(c) Used by vessel in distress or station designated to control the distress to announce that restricted working can resume. Typically allowing either Urgency or Safety broadcasts to be made.

(d) Used by a vessel to impose radio silence on another station during a distress. The vessel is not controlling the distress but has been alerted and is maintaining a watch.

8 Cargo: General Cargo – OOW Level

8.1 Some cargoes give off a strong odour that can be passed to, and taint, other substances. For example, tea, butter, rubber and eggs are liable to taint from other substances such as oranges and coffee.

8.2 Tea, butter, rubber and eggs are all susceptible to taint.

8.3 Oranges, coffee and fish are all likely to taint other cargoes.

8.4 Ship's sweat can occur when the temperature of the outside air is below the dew point of the air in the hold. This situation is likely to occur when a vessel passes from a warm to a colder climate, causing condensation on the ships hull.

8.5 Cargo sweat can occur when a vessel passes from a cool climate to a warmer one, the temperature of the hold cargo will be below the dew point of the outside air. If air is introduced into the hold condensation may form on the cargo surface.

8.6 Refer to the IMO 'Code of Safe Practice for Cargo Stowage and Securing' and vessel specific 'Cargo Securing Manual'.

8.7 Refer to the IMO 'Code of Safe Practice for Ships Carrying Timber Deck Cargoes'.

8.8 Hatch cover watertight integrity can be tested by:

- A chalk test of the hatch coaming against the rubber
- when hatches are secured - a hose test
- ultrasonic testing.

8.9 When working a forklift truck in a cargo hold:

- The truck should only be used by a competent person
- the truck should only be used when the ship is in still water and never used when the vessel is in a seaway
- vehicles powered by an internal combustion engine should not be used in an enclosed space.

8.10 Tank containers should not be lifted with the forks of a forklift because of the risk of instability and of damaging the container with the ends of the forks.

Forklift trucks fitted with suitably designed side or top lifting attachment may lift such tanks, but care must be taken.

8.11 If the vehicle is 'on deck stowage', it is important that each vehicle's fuel tank is not so full as to introduce a possibility of spillage.

If stowed 'under deck', not so full as to create spillage and the ignition is switched off.

8.12 Dunnaging should be fitted to keep the cargo clear of the deck by approximately 3 cms (approximately 5 cms for bags or bales). It should be laid athwartships to allow any water to drain to the scuppers.

8.13 Information on securing RoRo vehicles is found in:

- Vessel specific 'Cargo Securing Manual'
- Code of Safe Practice for Cargo Stowage and Securing (IMO)
- Guidelines for securing arrangements for the transport of road vehicles on RoRo ships (IMO Resolution A.581(14))
- M Notices (various).

8.14 No, reject the cargo container and inform the Chief Officer.

9 Cargo: Dangerous Goods – OOW Level

9.1 It is the lowest temperature at which the substance gives off sufficient vapours, such that when a lighted taper is applied near the surface, a flash across the surface of the substance will occur.

9.2 Dangerous goods include:

- Explosives
- gases
- inflammable liquids
- inflammable solids
- oxidising substances
- poisonous or infectious substances
- radioactive substances
- corrosives
- miscellaneous dangerous substances
- dangerous chemicals.

9.3 A volatile substance has a flashpoint below 60°C.

9.4 Auto ignition is the ignition of a combustible material, without initiation by a spark or flame, when the material has been raised to a temperature at which self-sustaining combustion occurs.

9.5 Spontaneous combustion is the ignition of material brought about by a heat producing chemical reaction within the material itself, without any exposure to an external source of ignition.

9.6 The label must survive for 3 months.

9.7 When loading dangerous goods:

- Reject any damaged or leaking packages
- cargo must be loaded in compliance with the ships DG 'Document of Compliance'
- DG declaration must be supplied
- Reject any unmarked cargo-without labels
- packages should be stowed in a protective location

- combustible material is to be kept away from ignition sources
- access provided to dangerous goods
- post signs and enforce 'No Smoking'.

9.8 Medical First Aid Guide, a supplement booklet to the IMDG Code, items/substances detailed by number from data sheet in this booklet and details of medical action to be administered.

9.9 Segregation varies by ship type, but can be referred by:

- Away from - 3 metres vertically
- separated from - separate compartment / on deck 6 metres apart
- separated by a complete hold or compartment / on deck 12 metres horizontal separation
- separated longitudinally by an intervening hold - 24 metres separation if on deck.

9.10 The IMDG Code provides product details including:

- Label of Class
- UN number
- chemical formula
- explosive limits
- properties
- observations
- packing instructions
- stowage
- packing, stowage and segregation.

9.11 The supplement to the IMDG Code contains:

- Medical First Aid Guide (MFAG)
- fire schedules
- spillage schedules
- reporting procedures
- international Code for the Safe Carriage of Packaged Irradiated Nuclear Fuel (INF) Code
- recommendations for the safe use of pesticides at sea.

10 Cargo: Bulk – OOW Level

10.1 Refer to the International Maritime Solid Bulk Cargoes Code (IMSBC).

10.2 Refer to the International Grain Code.

10.3 The carriage of coal requirements are referreds to in the IMSBC Code.

10.4 For a cargo, it is the amount or percentage of moisture required for a flow state to develop. This is found by experiment.

10.5 The following information should be provided for a bulk cargo:

- Angle of repose
- flow moisture point
- stowage factor
- actual moisture contents
- transportable moisture limit
- any dangers associated with the cargo.

10.6 Tests for hatch watertight integrity include:

- A chalk test of the hatch coaming against the rubber
- when hatches are secured - a hose test
- ultrasonic testing.

10.7 Grain includes:

- Wheat
- maize
- oats
- rye
- barley
- pulses
- seeds.

10.8 Before loading grain hold preparations should include:

- Ensuring that the space is clean, dry and free from odour

- bilges clean and free from odour
- an approved method must be employed to prevent grain entering bilges
- tank top must be free of stains and oil.

10.9 Partly-filled grain compartments can be secured by:

- Overstowing
- strapping or lashing
- use of wire mesh.

10.10 Moisture content in bulk cargoes is commonly caused by:

- Water associated with the manufacture of raw materials
- exposure to rain, snow or ice during loading, transporting to the ship or whilst in storage
- stockpiling on wet ground.

10.11 Hazards associated with coal include:

- Self heating, fire and explosion
- methane
- corrosivity
- carbon monoxide
- hydrogen can be produced by reacting with water
- liquefaction
- oxygen depletion.

10.12 After discharging coal and to prepare for loading grain:

- Space must be clean and free from odour
- bilges clean, strum boxes cleaned - coating of lime wash and cement wash
- bilge covers cleaned and covered with tarpaulins or burlap to prevent water entering bilges
- tank top clean and free from stains.

10.13 The IMSBC Code is comprised of:

- The IMSBC Code itself, which replaces the old BC Code, and
- 4 supplements containing:
    - BLU Code – Code of Safe Practice for the Safe Loading and Unloading of Bulk Carriers
    - BLU Manual – Manual on Loading of Solid Bulk Cargoes for Terminal Representatives
    - methods of measurement for bulk cargo density
    - list of Cargoes that do not need fire extinguishing systems or for which such systems would be ineffective
    - recommendations for enclosed space entry
    - recommendation on use of pesticides
    - contact details of responsible national authorities.

10.14 Iron and iron ore cargoes may be subject to oxidisation, and consequently oxygen depletion, and corrosion. Care needs to be taken due to its high density when loading to avoid damage to the ship's structure, excessive bending/shearing forces and excessive metacentric height (EM). Moisture content needs to be closely monitored.

11 Cargo: Oil – OOW Level

11.1 No, the sliding of a polypropylene rope through a PVC glove would pose an electrostatic hazard.

11.2 The advantage is its flexibility.

11.3 The disadvantages of the ringmain system are:

- Expensive
- slow loading
- high maintenance
- erosion in bends
- washing of lines is difficult.

11.4 The advantages of a direct line system are:

- Fast loading
- Segregation of cargo grades
- cheaper to build
- less maintenance required
- easier to operate.

11.5 The disadvantages of a direct line system are:

- Not very flexible
- problems due to lack of flexibility in event of valve failure.

11.6 The advantages of a free flow system are:

- Fast load/discharge of cargo
- very effective draining and stripping
- a very simple, low maintenance system.

11.7 The disadvantages of a free flow system are:

- Segregation is almost impossible
- problems if any fault develops
- may require a pipeline system for any sort of flexibility.

11.8 The advantages of cruciform system are:

- Versatile

- good segregation
- efficient and quick cargo load/discharge.

11.9 The disadvantages of a cruciform system are:

- Expensive to build
- maintenance is complex and expensive.

11.10 Advantages of crude oil washing:

- Increased cargo outturn
- reduced pre-drydock cleaning
- reduces pollution, through reduced decanting, etc
- reduces desludging time and cost
- reduction in tank cleaning on ballast passage
- less salt water discharged to terminal
- reduced deadfreight.

11.11 Disadvantages of crude oil washing:

- Increase in time at the discharge port
- increase in crew workload
- some loss of cargo due to vaporisation
- pollution risk due to complexity of COW line on deck
- reduces the bulk discharge rate.

11.12 Retained cargo residues can be disposed of by:

- Pumping residues ashore at the loading terminal
- retaining the residues onboard and loading the next cargo on top of them, dependent on compatability
- pumping the residues to a slop barge
- retaining the residues onboard, but separate from the new cargo.

11.13 Take the following actions:

- Stop loading
- raise the alarm
- tank opened to another tank with a greater ullage
- advise chief officer and master
- advise shore
- follow oil pollution response procedures (SOPEP).

11.14 Ensure that it is effectively bonded to prevent static discharge.

11.15 Delivery of inert gas must be less than 5% O_2.

11.16 O_2 content in the tank must remain below 8%

11.17 This procedure is called dilution.

11.18 A manual check should be made to ensure it is less than 8% by volume.

11.19 Personnel joining a tanker or similar vessel for the first time should receive:

- Basic safety induction to the main hazards associated with the vessel, before or on joining the vessel
- full job description
- information as specified in the ship's safety management system (SMS).

11.20 Volatile petroleum substances have a flashpoint below 60°C.

11.21 Non-volatile petroleum substances have a flashpoint above 60°C.

11.22 If rubbed across steel it leaves an aluminium smear and, if it is subsequently struck, it can cause an incendive spark.

11.23 Hydrogen Sulphide (H_2S) is a colourless vapour which is highly toxic and, if not managed correctly, potentially lethal. It is characterised by its distinctive odour of rotten eggs, which may be detected at vapour concentrations as low as 1 ppm. However, exposure to vapour concentrations in excess of 100 ppm can lead to a rapid loss of the sense of smell. At concentrations in excess of 500 ppm, the nerve centre in the brain is affected, resulting in a rapid loss of consciousness, following which there may be interruption of respiration due to depression of the respiratory centres of the brain.

11.24 Pressure/vacuum (P/V) relief valves prevent structural damage to cargo tanks caused by excessive pressure or vacuum.

12 Cargo: Chemicals – OOW Level

12.1 A 'Procedures & Arrangement' manual required under MARPOL Annex II.

12.2 Nitrogen (N_2) is the primary inerting medium used.

12.3 Nitrogen is particularly hazardous as it has no 'smell or odour'.

12.4 Fresh water showers and eyewash arrangements are available onboard.

12.5 Oxygen level should be manually tested to ensure it is less than 8% by volume.

12.6 First aid guidance that complements the data sheet is found in the Medical First Aid Guide.

12.7 Symptoms that indicate poisoning include:

- Unexpected headaches
- nausea and vomiting
- drowsiness
- change in mental behaviour
- unconsciousness
- convulsions of pain
- if the patient has a rapid but weak pulse, greyish blue colour of skin, severe breathing difficulty or remains unconscious for a prolonged period, severe poisoning must be suspected.

12.8 The most common corrosive substances carried onboard are acids and bases or alkalis.

12.9 The four main groups are:

- Petrochemicals
- alcohols and carbohydrates
- vegetable and animal oils and fats
- acids
- inorganic chemicals.

12.10 Putrefaction is the process when organic material decomposes.

12.11 No. A ship/shore bonding cable is not effective as a safety device and may be dangerous. A ship/shore bonding cable should not be used.

12.12 Inert gas (IG) guidance can be found in:

- The International Safety Guide for Oil Tankers and Terminals (ISGOTT)
- IMO's Inert Gas Systems publication
- manufacturer guidelines.

12.13 Inert gas must be produced at the source at less than 5% oxygen by volume.

12.14 Inert gas must remain below 8% oxygen by volume in the cargo tanks.

12.15 The term used to describe this method of inerting is 'dilution'.

12.16 Threshold limit value which can be expressed as a STEL - short term exposure limit, TWA - time weighted average or C – ceiling.

12.17 SOPEP is the Shipboard Oil Pollution Emergency Plan which may on chemical tankers form part of the P&A Manual.

13 Cargo: LPG – OOW Level

13.1 Fresh water showers and eyewash arrangements.

13.2 Information would be available in the Medical First Aid Guide.

13.3 The chemical symbol for Ammonia is NH_3.

13.4 Deepwell pumps are normally used on LPG ships.

13.5 Sulzer or Linde are among those commonly used.

13.6 Tank volume limits are 98% (0.98).

13.7 The term used to describe retained cargo for tank cooling is 'Heel'.

13.8 Ammonia vapour is lighter than air.

13.9 LPG vapour is heavier than air.

13.10 No. Canister or filter type respirators should never be used in enclosed spaces where the oxygen level is insufficient to sustain life. In such a situation, Self Contained Breathing Apparatus should be used.

14 Cargo: LNG – OOW Level

14.1 Four types of containment systems:

- Gaz Transport membrane
- Technigaz membrane
- Kvaerner Moss spherical - independent Type 'B'
- IHI SPB Tank - prismatic.

14.2 Daily boil-off rates during the loaded voyage vary with changes in barometric pressure - unless absolute pressure control is adopted, ambient temperature and sea conditions. For this reason, a close watch must be kept on tank pressures and inter-barrier space pressures. On no account should cargo tank pressures be allowed to fall below atmospheric.

14.3 Shaft seals are normally pressurised with nitrogen.

14.4 The other gases have densities heavier than air and are therefore deemed to be too hazardous for this purpose.

14.5 A nitrogen generation plant.

14.6 It allows very low pump-down levels to be achieved.

14.7 The boil-off vapours are usually fed to the ship's boilers, via a compressor and heater, for use as main propulsion fuel.

14.8 These are used on the ballast voyage to minimise tank thermal gradients in addition to cooling down requirements.

14.9 Lower Flammable Limit for CH_4 (LFL) is 5%.

Upper Flammable Limit (UFL) for CH_4 is 14%.

14.10 The specific gravity (SG) of LNG varies slightly regarding quality, ie actual CH_4 content, but can on average be taken as 0.46, less than half the weight of water.

14.11 At the phase change from liquid to vapour, LNG undergoes a volumetric expansion of approximately 600-620x, ie a small amount of trapped liquid can result in an extremely high pressure.

14.12 At normal atmosheric pressure and temperature the actual boiling point of LNG is taken as minus 158.9°C.

14.13 Gauge Pressure is the value of pressure above atmospheric pressure.

Absolute Pressure is the value of pressure above Zero, ie Gauge Pressure + Atmospheric Pressure.

14.14 The white plume visible when LNG vapour vents is caused by the condensing water vapour in the atmosphere. As a rough guide the limits of flammability of the cloud are the same as the visible limits.

14.15 At sea (ballast) tank pressure at any time should never be allowed to fall below approximately 1083 mbar (Abs) or 70 mbar (Gauge). This keeps membrane fatigue stresses within maker's recommended values.

14.16 The closing time of the manifold valves is 25 to 30 sec. This closing time allowance prevents the build up of 'surge' in the lines, in particular preventing damage to the loading arms.

14.17 When inerting (LNG to IG), the operation must be continued until the hydrocarbon content has been reduced to 1.6% by volume or less.

14.18 Before personnel can enter a cargo tank the chemist (and the ship) must test for Carbon-monoxide (50ppm), Carbon-dioxide (5000ppm) & Hydrogen Sulphide.

14.19 The hazards posed by water ingress into the insulated space are: ice deformation, head press damage, possible secondary membrane rupture, and so establishing a cold path.

07574913565